Getting into

Oxford & Cambridge

2016 entry

Seán P. Buckley

18th edition

Getting into guides

Getting into Art & Design Courses, 9th edition
Getting into Business & Economics Courses, 11th edition
Getting into Dental School, 9th edition
Getting into Engineering Courses, 3rd edition
Getting into Law, 10th edition
Getting into Medical School: 2016 entry, 20th edition
Getting into Pharmacy and Pharmacology Courses, 1st edition
Getting into Physiotherapy Courses, 7th edition
Getting into Psychology Courses, 10th edition
Getting into Veterinary School, 10th edition
How to Complete Your UCAS Application: 2016 entry, 27th edition

Getting into Oxford & Cambridge: 2016 Entry

This 18th edition published in 2015 by Trotman Education, an imprint of Crimson Publishing Ltd, 19–21c Charles Street, Bath BA1 1HX

© Trotman Education 2008, 2009, 2010, 2011, 2012, 2013, 2014, 2015

© Trotman & Co Ltd 1987, 1989, 1991, 1994, 1996, 1999, 2001, 2003, 2005, 2007

Author: Seán P. Buckley

17th edition by Seán P. Buckley; editions 15–16 by Jenny Blaiklock; editions 13–14 by Katy Blatt; 12th edition by Sarah Alakija; 11th edition by Natalie Lancer; editions 7–10 by Sarah Alakija.

Tables 2,3 and 4 reproduced with the permission of the Chancellor, Master and Scholars of the University of Oxford.

British Library Cataloguing in Publication Data
A catalogue record for this book is available from the British Library

ISBN: 978 1 909319 63 9

Typeset by IDSUK (DataConnection) Ltd
Printed and bound in the UK by TJ International Ltd, Padstow, Cornwall

Contents

About the author

Seán Buckley read English and English Literature at Lady Margaret Hall, Oxford. Subsequently, he was awarded his PhD in the field of nineteenth-century Irish writing by the University of London. He has been teaching for almost 30 years and is currently Academic Director International at Mander Portman Woodward College in London. In addition to his duties at MPW, he is a senior examiner at one of the main examination boards.

Seán is married with four children and spends as much of his free time as possible at his family home in Ireland.

Acknowledgements

I am indebted to Ciáran Buckley, who conducted much of the research. Special thanks to those generous Oxbridge students who donated their personal statements and written case studies. Thanks are also due to those colleagues who helped me update reading lists in their subject areas.

I dedicate this book to my young cousin, Tim O'Donoghue, who died in 2014.

Foreword

I was one of the first, if not the first, of my large extended family to go to university. Certainly, I was in the first generation of my family to benefit from tertiary education. For example, my father left school at 13 to work on the family farm before emigrating to England, while my mother left school at 17 to emigrate to London to become a nurse. It is a testament to their lifelong love of learning, despite their lack of college or university education, that I was able to lay the foundations for my own academic success.

I had not originally intended to go to university. Having worked on building sites during my holidays since the age of 15, I was fully prepared to follow my father into a life in the construction industry after my A levels. It was my headmaster, a Jesuit priest, who first suggested I could be a contender for the University of Oxford, when he rang my home out of the blue to discuss my A level results. Times have changed; in those days it seemed to be enough to have done exceptionally well in the subject you were likely to read at university, rather than having the equivalent of the A*AA or A*A*A grades students need nowadays.

My school, which sent one or two students a year to Oxford or Cambridge, was very accommodating and supportive. They gave me a few hours a week of individual tuition, alongside my work on the building site, to prepare me for what was called seventh-term entry. These lessons, taught enthusiastically and inspirationally by Father Alf Thomas, gave me a taste for the type and style of study that I would later encounter at Oxford: close reading, analysis and interpretation of literary texts. I went on to pass the university entrance test and survived my series of interviews which was, in retrospect, also quite enjoyable.

It was more a feeling of relief that I experienced when I learned I had been given an unconditional offer to read English Language and Literature at Lady Margaret Hall, Oxford. I did not really know what to expect at university, not having any close relatives or friends with any university experience. Instead, I prepared by immersing myself in the English faculty's recommended reading list; my reading during breaks was tolerated and even encouraged by my workmates on the building site.

Needless to say, my parents were very proud of my achievement in securing a place at Oxford, a pride that was augmented when my younger brother won a place at New College, Oxford the following year.

I wanted to give you an insight into my background as I am keen to convey the idea that Oxford and Cambridge universities are not just bastions of one particular type of undergraduate. While it may be argued that students from more privileged backgrounds stand a statistically greater chance of gaining an Oxbridge place, there is room for students from all backgrounds who are passionate about their subject, who have solid academic foundations and who can demonstrate the potential to succeed on their degree courses at Oxford or Cambridge.

I remember with fondness my time at Oxford. Lady Margaret Hall is set in beautiful riverside grounds; it was a privilege to study there. Having friends at other colleges and organising events in venues other than LMH meant that I gained a broader perspective of the university as a whole. Continuing to work on building sites during the six months of the year that was not devoted to university study ensured that I was financially solvent; this was considered rare at the time and is perhaps even rarer now, with student loans having replaced the student grants which were awarded in those days. What I really appreciated was the opportunity to indulge my love of literature; perhaps I appreciate it even more now that there are competing demands on my time. My advice to those of you who are successful in your Oxbridge applications – and I hope most of you are – is to make the most of these special places and the time you spend there.

There are so many other things to get involved in at university, especially at Oxford and Cambridge. Personally, I was active in the literary society, the Labour club and the boxing club, which all enriched my university experience. Most memorably, I was a founder member and the first secretary of the Oxford University Irish Society. This involved promoting Irish culture within the university on occasions such as the Freshers' Fair, establishing links with the broader Irish community and planning events such as musical concerts, talks by visiting speakers and art exhibitions. I really felt I was part of something at this time and I was fully supported by my college and university in this endeavour.

Last May, I returned to my alma mater for the launch of the Hetherington Society, a charity founded in memory of a former LMH student and renowned war photographer, Tim Hetherington, who was killed while on an assignment in Libya. Not only was I impressed by the event itself, but I was also struck by the demeanour of the many undergraduates present. It was clear that they were public spirited, articulate and passionate about their subjects. It is very much to be hoped that you too will soon be such a student at whichever Oxford or Cambridge college you attend.

Partly in order to redress the balance in favour of Cambridge, having written so much about Oxford in the previous edition of the introduction, I visited Cambridge on a number of occasions during the autumn of 2014. All three occasions were to do with students at various stages on their educational journey, which is of special interest to those readers considering the next stage of their academic life. One visit was an examiners' meeting for IGCSE. Another one was accompanying a party of new students from overseas as they embarked on their AS studies. They visited Sidney Sussex College and benefited from a very informative talk from the admissions officer as well as being inspired by some of the students who acted as guides. The third visit was to discuss international A level students at my sister college in Cambridge before travelling to see their parents in China. While in Cambridge, of course, I saw the sights that enthral tourists: at King's I watched cattle grazing in the meadow across the River Cam, along which punts gently glided past in the late afternoon sun in October. Somewhat stereotypically, I also observed some of the 'high jinks' that may characterise Cambridge in some people's eyes, such as two students jumping from a bridge into a punt waiting below, to the applause of the onlookers at The Anchor public house. However, I was also impressed by how rich and varied life at Cambridge can be. Just to give you a musical snapshot, in the space of a few hours on a Saturday afternoon I attended an organ recital at Queen's College and a Vivaldi concert at Trinity College. The evening before it was refreshing to see the 'freshers' enjoying themselves at their matriculation dinners in a range of colleges. As I entered the great wooden gate of one college, I stepped aside to let an undergraduate dressed as a cat pass by; thirty more 'cats' followed the first one.

As I mentioned earlier, I was travelling to China the following week. Because of this and because of the provenance of the students I have been looking after, the international dimension of Cambridge loomed large for me and overseas students will be interested in the following pages, as well as home students. This international connection has always been important for Cambridge and of course Cambridge, as well as Oxford, has an international reputation. It was interesting to see the exhibition in King's College Chapel about Xu Zhimo from Haining in Zhejiang, a province in China I was to visit the following week. Xu Zhimo was a Chinese poet who stayed in Cambridge from 1921 to 1922 and who drew comparisons in his poetry between Cambridge colleges along the Cam and his home town. Two of the Chinese students from my college matriculated at Cambridge that week, so I found the connection especially significant.

Introduction

The title of this book says it all. Its purpose is to tell you everything you need to know to help you get into Oxford or Cambridge. It will also try to give you a flavour of what it's like to study there. My hope is that this book will help to demystify the whole application process and encourage you to apply if you feel you've got what it takes to get in.

You may already know quite a lot about the Oxbridge system and simply need a checklist of things you should do to ensure your best entry. This book certainly aims to be as comprehensive as possible and will cover all stages of the admissions procedure in detail.

You may know nothing at all about how to get in. Many potential applicants can be put off applying on the basis that Oxford or Cambridge somehow isn't right for them and that the odds of getting in are weighted towards students who have knowledge of a mythical 'old boys' network'. You would be wrong if you believe this. It is simply not true that Oxbridge operates in favour of those students who can somehow play the system. I have spoken to many admissions tutors in researching this book, and I can guarantee that your application will be judged, more than ever before, on your potential to succeed and your willingness to work hard. The school you went to, how much money you have and how many of your ancestors went to Oxford or Cambridge count for nothing; getting in is about your academic potential alone.

You also shouldn't be dissuaded because you're worried that you're not a geeky Oxbridge type or that you're somehow not posh enough to hold your own there. Perhaps with all the publicity about the government wanting to encourage applications from state school pupils, you're worried that your application will be prejudiced because you go to an independent school. You shouldn't be concerned about this either. Both universities are keen to encourage applications from academically talented students whatever their background. If you're passionate about your subject and have the ability to excel at university, you're almost certainly a strong candidate for admission.

The aim of this book is to take you through the application process step by step: from making sure you're studying the right A levels in the first instance to giving you tips to help you sail through your interview.

Chapter 1, What studying at Oxbridge is really like, explores why Oxford and Cambridge are so special and how they differ from other universities, giving the reader some idea of what it's like to study there.

It also aims to demystify the selection process by outlining Oxbridge's equal opportunities policy. It explains the policy for disabled students; students with children; students from ethnic minorities; lesbian, gay and bisexual students; and educationally disadvantaged students or students who have had a disrupted education.

Chapter 2, Money matters, explains the financial aspects of studying at Oxbridge. Many students are put off by the idea that studying at Oxbridge is more expensive than at other universities. This chapter explains that this is not the case, and gives a breakdown of costs incurred over a year. The chapter also introduces the bursary schemes and music scholarships at the universities, and includes a case study of the spending habits of a new student at Cambridge.

Chapter 3, Entry requirements, discusses things you should consider well before the UCAS application. The chapter includes a section on choosing your A level subjects and the concept of 'facilitating' A levels. It also discusses the importance of high grades and the alternatives to UK A levels that are accepted by Oxford and Cambridge (including the Baccalaureate and Scottish Highers).

Chapter 4, Early stages of preparation, discusses the importance of choosing the right subject for you. Your choice of subject is more important than any other decision you will have to make during this process; more important than your choice of university and college. This chapter looks at the workload placed on students and the need to be prepared for this by reading widely and in depth. Also included in this section is a reading list that will give you a few ideas.

Chapter 5, Choosing your university and college, considers the best way to choose a university and college. It mentions the differences between Oxford and Cambridge, highlighting the importance of choosing the university that offers the subject that most suits you. Although this chapter refers to the Norrington and Tompkins tables as points of reference (see Appendix 3), it advises against a tactical approach to college choice. Instead, it offers alternative methods for picking your future home. This chapter also explains the option of the 'open application'.

Chapter 6, Experience to support your UCAS application, discusses the importance of extracurricular experience in the application process. The option of a 'gap year' is considered, and how this 'time out' can be advantageous in some circumstances but disadvantageous in others. It looks at the importance of work experience, particularly if you wish to study a vocational subject at university, and how essential it is to be aware of events in your area, current affairs and news stories that are relevant to your chosen subject.

Chapter 7, The UCAS application and the personal statement, gives advice on UCAS and the personal statement. Suggestions are offered on how to make your application shine, as well as example statements with analysis. After you have completed your personal statement, Cambridge (but not Oxford) automatically sends a Supplementary Application Questionnaire (SAQ), and this chapter also gives advice on how to fill in this form. Many subjects require you to send in examples of written work and this section explains why written work is required, for which subjects essay submissions are usual and how best to satisfy the universities' requirements.

Chapter 8, Succeeding in written tests, discusses the exams that are taken in addition to A levels for some subjects. These are taken either in advance of interviews or during the interview week in order to help interviewers decide on the best applicants. This chapter explains why these tests are necessary; gives lists of the subjects requiring additional testing at both Oxford and Cambridge; gives example questions, dates for testing and useful website links; and provides reading lists so that you can find out more for yourself.

Chapter 9, Surviving the interview, explains the interview process. General information about interview practice is given, as well as a breakdown of what interviewers are looking for. In addition, there is information about different interview styles and how to deal with them; a comprehensive list of interview questions for a range of subjects; and six interview stories from previous applicants. Finally, there is a word of advice about presentation skills and an explanation of the pooling system.

Chapter 10, Non-standard applications, discusses the application procedure for mature students and international students and gives information on specific issues relating to these categories.

Chapter 11, Getting the letter, looks at the final stages of the process: receiving an offer or coping with rejection; stress; and how you can make this experience a success, whether or not you obtain a place at Oxbridge.

In the appendices you will find: a useful timeline of the application process; a glossary of important terms; the Norrington and Tompkins tables; and, finally, maps of both Oxford and Cambridge with the locations of the colleges marked.

Throughout the book, the examples that quote university entrance requirements use A level and AS level grades. However, the advice is applicable to students studying Scottish Highers, the International Baccalaureate, Pre-University (Pre-U) and other qualifications. The UCAS website (www.ucas.com) lists entrance requirements for all of the major examination systems in its 'Course Search' section. If you are unsure about what you need to achieve, individual universities will be happy to give you advice; contact details are given on all of their websites.

1 | What studying at Oxford and Cambridge is really like

If you are considering an application to Oxford or Cambridge, you are probably keen to understand what makes these two universities such special places to study and why places are so fiercely fought over. This chapter will explain what sets Oxford and Cambridge apart from other universities and examines the advantages and disadvantages of studying there.

Previous editions of this guide have talked about eminent and famous Oxford and Cambridge alumni, such as British prime ministers, international leaders, Nobel prize winners and so on. Clearly, there are excellent, aspirational places of study, known the world over. However, so much else can and does go on at these universities. For the sports fans reading this book, I shall give one example of an Oxford student who managed to combine his academic pursuits with his sporting prowess, with not a little success. Cuthbert Ottaway was a student at Brasenose College, Oxford, reading Classics when he became the first captain of England in the first-ever official international soccer fixture, against Scotland in 1872. Incidentally, he also captained the Oxford University Cricket Club against Cambridge while he was a student. This serves as one example to show that the determined, motivated and well-rounded undergraduates that universities such as Oxford and Cambridge value can balance their studies with other activities.

What is important is that Oxford and Cambridge are at the forefront of academic excellence. It is also important to note that both Oxford and Cambridge produce rates of graduate employment which are amongst the highest in the UK.

Why study at Oxford or Cambridge?

Oxford and Cambridge are always top of the university league tables

In 2014 the *Guardian* ran a survey that ranked UK universities according to teaching excellence (see www.theguardian.com/education/ng-interactive/2014/jun/02/university-league-tables-2015-the-complete-list).

Cambridge topped the league table, with Oxford holding on to second place. The tables rank universities according to the following measures:

- how satisfied their final-year students are
- how much they spend per student
- the student–staff ratio
- the career prospects of their graduates
- a value-added score and what grades pupils have to achieve to stand a chance of being offered a place.

The tutorial system

Unlike most universities, teaching at Oxford and Cambridge is built around the tutorial system. Tutorials (or supervisions as they are called at Cambridge) involve a meeting with your tutor, alone or with one or two other students, and generally last about an hour. Often, one of you will read your essay or written work aloud and this will act as a catalyst for discussion of the work that has been done independently during the week.

What makes an Oxbridge education so special is that you will have personal access to some of the world's experts in your chosen subject. Your tutor may be the person who actually 'wrote the book' on the subject you're studying, so being able to discuss topics with them in depth every week is an invaluable experience.

Case study: Kapish, Oxford

Reading PPE at Oxford was one of the most challenging and rewarding experiences of my life. The degree requires a momentous commitment towards academic study, both in terms of intensity and the quantity of work involved. The degree itself, and Oxford generally, provides you with an inimitable set of skills and an outlook on life which are not only enduring, but also highly sought after. For me, the rewards were a radically sharpened analytical ability, acquiring resourceful working patterns, and new, higher goals.

One of the prime benefits of the degree is acquiring the ability to think critically about any issue, from a complex mathematical problem to a controversial policy issue. No assumption is unquestioned. Indeed, by the end of the degree it becomes second nature to analyse everything from 'the ground up', the Cartesian way. The result of this is that you end up coming up with ideas and solutions which are often highly effective but extremely simple. This skill is honed repetitively during weekly hour-long tutorials with a leading academic in the relevant field of study and another student taking the same paper. The tutorials are the 'engine room' of an Oxford education as it is during tutorials that the students learn how to put forward their own viewpoint, defend their analysis, and indeed quash their peers' arguments.

The tutorials (and examinations) require the extensive study of several works in a relatively short space of time, from classic and modern texts to the latest journal articles, across all the modules in the degree. Indeed, the term-time work entails writing at least two 2,000-word essays on a weekly basis, which are the focus of the tutorials. This routine forces you to become significantly more productive and efficient with your time, training you to become a skilled hunter of the necessary information and ideas from the dense volumes of text. This capacity to multi-task and work industriously is universally applicable and allows you to do more – be it work or extra-curricular activities – in less time.

An important feature of Oxford is that you are surrounded by some of the best minds in the world – be they your tutors or your peers – who constantly inspire you with new ideas, their person-alities and, indeed, their lifestyle choices. People around you often seem unafraid to try new things, to challenge themselves and to pack more extra-curricular activities into an already limited schedule. This not only means that you are pushed by 'soft' peer pressure to take on more challenges, it also means that you dis-cover facets and skills in your personality you thought you never had. For me, this meant participating in debating and student political organisations, standing for elections, and taking up golf. But more pertinently, this constant need to challenge yourself also takes a more profound form when you start setting yourself much higher goals than before.

This triad of heightened analytical ability, focused industry and superior goals forms a formidable combination, for which I have my Oxford education to thank. A perhaps more tangible result of attaining these skills is your increased worth in the labour market after graduation. Suffice it to say that my degree has allowed me to explore various career opportunities which would not have been available without it.

Case Study: Sam, St Hugh's College, Oxford

After finishing high school in Australia, I moved to Oxford to study mathematics, partially because my elder sister studied overseas, and partially due to the university's academic reputation. Being at Oxford was a great opportunity to immerse myself in my subject – it was one of the first times in my life where I could have proper conversations about mathematics with my friends – as well as getting to know a lot of other people with similar passions for their own subjects. I also really enjoyed living in college at St Hugh's, where I became actively involved in the football team and had the opportunity to forge strong friendships with fellow students. My time at Oxford offered a unique chance to wholeheartedly pursue my studies, as well as enjoy myself with like-minded people, and I left feeling fully assured that I had made the right decision in choosing to go there.

Case study: Florence, Cambridge

My first year reading geography was relatively hectic. I had on average two lectures a day and I had practical sessions every week that involved statistics and GIS modelling. Compared to A levels, it was a lot more work and I worked on essays every week. I had to be very organised and made sure I attended every lecture. The supervision system is great, because you can ask questions on things you haven't understood. My supervisors are very helpful and have given me a lot of exam advice. Overall, the most stressful time was Easter term when we had exams. Having said that, the whole experience has been really rewarding and I am settling in well into my second year of study.

The colleges

Oxford and Cambridge colleges are an integral part of both universities. They are independent, self-governing communities of academics, students and staff.

The collegiate system is one of their strengths, giving students and academics the benefits of belonging both to a large, internationally renowned institution and to a smaller, interdisciplinary, academic college community. Colleges and halls enable leading academics and students across subjects and year groups, and from different cultures and countries, to come together and share ideas. Membership of an Oxbridge college, as well as a department or faculty, can add a whole new dimension to your university experience.

Your college can provide you with the perfect forum to discuss your work in seminars, over meals in the dining hall or in your room late into the evening. It will help you to make friends quickly, and give you the opportunity to try a wide range of social and sporting activities.

All colleges invest heavily in facilities for library and IT provision, accommodation and pastoral care, and offer sports and social events. Undergraduate students benefit from the junior common room (JCR) in their college – both a physical space and an organisation, it provides social events, advice and a link to the undergraduate community.

The relatively small number of students at each college means that you receive plenty of personal academic support. Each student has a college adviser, who is a member of the college's academic staff and who looks after the students throughout their time at college.

The standard of accommodation and food offered by some colleges is generally superior to that offered by most UK universities. Certain colleges have Michelin-starred chefs overseeing their kitchens, and wine cellars that equal those of some of the best clubs in the world. Unlike most universities, many colleges can accommodate you for the whole of your time at university, saving you the trouble and expense of finding your own accommodation.

The best libraries and research facilities

Oxford and Cambridge are consistently placed among the highest-ranked universities for their research performance and have been shown to outperform UK competitors in the scale and quality of their research across a wide range of subject areas.

The two universities also far outstrip other universities in terms of income from endowments and other private sources because of their age and their ability to attract funds from alumni and other donors.

Oxbridge students have access to the Bodleian (Oxford) and the Fitzwilliam (Cambridge) copyright libraries, which hold a copy of every book, pamphlet, journal and magazine ever published in the UK. They are also non-lending, so students can always access the texts they need quickly, no matter how obscure. There are also hundreds of other libraries in Oxford and Cambridge, including at least one for each faculty and college.

The people you'll meet

Contrary to popular belief, people who study at Oxford and Cambridge come from very diverse backgrounds and have many different interests and personalities. There really is no such thing as an 'Oxbridge type'. If you enjoy art, music, sport, acting, drinking, clubbing or just about any sort of activity imaginable, there will be many like-minded soul mates waiting to share your interests. Students come from private schools, state schools and from overseas. It's up to you to decide whether you want to spend your time punting along the river, attending May balls, writing for the university magazines, speaking at the Students' Union, drinking in the JCR, or none of these things. Your Oxbridge experience is one only you can create; forget the clichés.

It is true, however, that Oxford and Cambridge attract the highest-performing undergraduate students, so you will be keeping company with some of the brightest people in the country and from abroad. They may not all become your friends or be your type but you are sure to find their company stimulating and intellectually satisfying.

The location

Both Oxford and Cambridge are undeniably beautiful places to live and each has its own very special character.

Cambridge is much smaller than Oxford and has a market-town feel about it. The university buildings are set much closer together, with a few exceptions such as Girton. Oxford feels more like a university set inside a city; colleges and faculty buildings are spaced out over a wider area and you will probably need a bike to get around easily.

Both universities have many beautiful buildings and each has its own architectural integrity. The colleges are stunning, whether you're into ancient architecture or modern chrome and glass.

Case study: Stephanie, Queen's College, Cambridge

I hadn't originally planned to go to a university like Oxford or Cambridge, certainly not until I has got well into my AS year. I had many friends and relations who had gone to other universities and had enjoyed their experiences, so I was more interested in those universities at first.

However, as I continued to get very good grades during my AS course, having already got mostly A* grades at GCSE, some of my teachers suggested that I might like to try to get into Oxford or Cambridge. We hadn't really had many students at our school who had applied to either university, so the teachers did not have much experience of preparing students for entry, but they gave me prospectuses, told me which websites to look at and encouraged me to have confidence in applying.

I really liked the natural sciences course at Cambridge, which was the main reason why I applied. I manage to get some wider experience helping out in a lab, which really reinforced my decision to apply for science-related subjects at university and to the natural sciences course in particular. I also did a research project, which was not only very interesting in itself, but enhanced my personal statement when I wrote about my research in detail.

I visited Cambridge informally during the summer after my AS examinations. I really liked the look of Queen's College, because of its location and mix of architecture. Although I did not know anyone there, I decided to apply to Queen's. I worked hard on my UCAS application during the rest of the summer, having looked at some samples that one of my teachers provided, and I was ready to apply by early September.

I was successful in my interview, which I had prepared for by practising with some of my tutors as well as with my friends and family. This was just to help me get over my nerves. I was careful not to over-prepare, as I did not want to feel that I rehearsed too much when I was in the interview. This was just as well, because while I was asked some questions about what I had said in my personal statement, I was asked other questions which I had not expected. Fortunately, I was able to think on my feet and my firm grounding in my subjects, my research and my work experience helped me a great deal.

It is very hard work here, but I am really enjoying it. I have joined several clubs and I also keep myself fit by cycling around college. Although I did not know anyone when I came here, I have become firm friends with quite a number of people, both at Queen's and at other colleges.

Employers are impressed by an Oxbridge degree

While having a First Class degree will improve your employment prospects more than anything else, employers are always impressed by an Oxbridge degree. The tutorial system will have taught you many useful skills: how to formulate and articulate a logical point of view, how to work independently, how to assimilate large amounts of information and how to prepare for tight deadlines. Oxbridge graduates have the confidence, intellect and skills that employers are looking for.

It can also be easier to get an internship while you're studying at Oxbridge because the university terms are shorter and can be fitted around relevant work experience, and, if travel is your thing, you'll have long vacations in which to explore the world.

Case study: Priya, Pembroke College, Cambridge

I have been working hard on preparing for applying for internships for a few months and my hard work has started to reap some rewards. I would really like to get into law eventually, but at the moment I am aiming for internships in a number of companies that are not related to law, just to build up experience. The hard work comes with the amount of applications you have to make for good internships and the fact that, increasingly, you can't just send out standard letters for internships but you have to tailor each letter very carefully for each employer. In addition, you mostly have to do online tests for good internships – and even for not so good ones – so preparing for these and completing them can take up a lot of time.

The difficulty at the moment is that there is a lot of competition, even for internships. Sometimes I feel that it is almost as competitive as the job market; at other times, I feel it is even more competitive! However, the skills I have learned at Cambridge – I mean the people skills, the time-management skills and so on rather than the knowledge I am acquiring for my degree – have been invaluable. I have also been lucky enough to have regular paid work as a receptionist each summer holiday, so that has given me a bit of extra experience and has given me more life skills.

When I have got to interview, I think the fact that I am at Cambridge does impress prospective employers and the confidence I have got in articulating myself effectively from my supervisions is really helpful too.

Are there any disadvantages?

The eight-week terms make your studying time very intensive and you will have to work hard outside term time too. Some students find the atmosphere highly pressured; you will constantly be called upon to meet deadlines and assimilate large amounts of information in a very short time. You will also have to balance your extracurricular activities alongside your demanding academic schedule.

Neither of the universities allows undergraduate students to take on part-time work (which should be taken into consideration when you're planning your finances), although there may be limited opportunities for paid employment within the college, for example in the libraries or JCR.

Some people will tell you that Oxford and Cambridge are not good places to go if you want to play masses of sport or be in a band or basically do anything other than study. It is certainly difficult to strike the right balance but many fine sportsmen and women, musicians, actors, artists and novelists have managed to do just that.

Will it be suitable for me?

Just because Cambridge and Oxford are two of the leading universities in the world, this does not mean that you should be daunted by their reputations. Their sole criterion for accepting new undergraduates is academic excellence. This is assessed through academic qualifications, during interviews and through special written tests prior to or during the interview stage. If you have good academic qualifications and are passionate about learning, you are eligible and they will welcome your application.

Students with disabilities and special educational needs (SEN)

Students with disabilities and SEN students are welcome at both universities and are in no way disadvantaged in their application. Disabilities must be declared on the UCAS form in order for the university and college to pool their resources and you must contact the admissions office at university and college level to discuss your individual needs.

For students with physical disabilities and impaired movement, living in older colleges can be tricky. Because Oxford and Cambridge are so old, much of the architecture is 'listed', making it illegal to make changes to the buildings in any way. This means that it is sometimes impossible to install lifts. The same is true of some faculties, for example the architecture faculty at Cambridge. There are, however, many faculties with new buildings that do not pose such problems, and several colleges in both universities have recently been renovated. You will need to consult your chosen college to advise you on whether it is able to accommodate your needs.

Students with dyslexia are given the opportunity to write using a computer and extra time during exams; they should feel in no way anxious about applying. Those with visual or hearing impairments are also welcome to apply.

Each college should have a member of staff responsible for disabled students. You should ring the admissions tutor at your chosen college who will put you in touch with the disability staff member to discuss its resources and your needs. Students can also apply for the Disabled Students Allowance (DSA). Cambridge offers more advice on this on www.admin.cam.ac.uk/univ/disability/students/finance/funding/dsa/html while more information about the DSA at Oxford can be found at www.ox.ac.uk/students/welfare/disability/funding. For more information in general, look at the Cambridge Disability Resource Centre at www.admin.cam.ac.uk/univ/disability, or the Oxford University Disability Advisory Service at www.admin.ox.ac.uk/eop/disab.

Students with children

Both Oxford and Cambridge welcome applications from prospective students who have children. Several colleges provide accommodation for couples and families and some colleges have their own nurseries. They each also have a university-wide nursery. You should ring the admissions office at your chosen college for more information.

UK students at both universities can ask to be considered for a university and college hardship fund (www.gov.uk/extra-money-pay-university/ university-and-college-hardship-funds). Students should contact the student services department at their university to see if they are eligible. Students with children, especially single parents, could qualify as students with children are one of the priority groups for support. More information is available at the following websites:

- Cambridge: www.admin.cam.ac.uk/students/studentregistry/fees/ funding/hardship/atl.html
- Oxford: www.admin.ox.ac.uk/childcare/feesandfunding
- www.gov.uk/access-to-learning-fund/overview.

The 'Cambridge Guide for Student Parents' is written yearly by the Cambridge University Students' Union (CUSU) and is available online at www.cusu.cam.ac.uk/welfare/childcare. Some colleges are also members of the Central Childcare Bursary Scheme that offers means-tested grants to overseas and EU students to help with the costs of childcare. This is not a loan and does not need to be repaid. Application forms are available from college offices, the childcare information adviser and CUSU. Applications can be made at any time during the academic year.

Oxford University provides similar support, heavily subsidising the cost of local nursery care, as well as funding holiday play schemes. See www.admin.ox.ac.uk/childcare for further details. Oxford University Student Union (OUSU) provides useful information on childcare, funding and other necessities for students who are also parents (http:// ousu.org/advice/life-welfare/student-parents).

Students from ethnic minorities

It must be said that the number of students from ethnic minorities at Oxbridge is low. This has generated a large amount of bad press for both universities, perhaps undeservedly. Statistics show that the percentage of minority applicants accepted out of those who apply is very similar to the percentage of white Western applicants who are successful. This suggests that the cause of under-representation of ethnic minorities is primarily due to the lack of applications from these groups rather than a bias against them, and both universities have outreach policies that aim to attract students from under-represented groups.

Cambridge University states in its Equal Opportunity Policy and Codes of Practice that:

> 'The University of Cambridge is committed in its pursuit of academic excellence to equality of opportunity and to a pro-active and inclusive approach to equality, which supports and encourages all under-represented groups, promotes an inclusive culture, and values diversity . . . [The University promises to] monitor the recruitment and progress of all students . . . paying particular attention to the recruitment and progress of ethnic minority students and staff.'
>
> www.admin.cam.ac.uk/offices/hr/policy/equal.html

In its Race Equality Policy, Oxford University states that:

> 'The University of Oxford welcomes diversity amongst its students . . . recognising the contributions to the achievement of the University's mission that can be made by individuals from a wide range of backgrounds and experiences. The University aims to provide an inclusive environment which promotes equality, values diversity and maintains a working, learning and social environment in which the rights and dignity of all its . . . students are respected to assist them in reaching their full potential. The University will work to remove any barriers which might deter people of the highest potential and ability from applying to Oxford, either as staff or students.'
>
> www.admin.ox.ac.uk/eop/race/policy

Lesbian, gay, bisexual and transsexual (LGBT) students

Oxford and Cambridge are pluralist universities. Not only is there a central LGBT society at each university but each college also has its own LGBT representative. There are plenty of events to help you feel comfortable. For further information have a look at these websites:

- Cambridge: LGBT information from CUSU: www.lgbt.cusu.cam.ac.uk
- Oxford: LGBTQ Council at Oxford University Student Union (OUSU): www.oulgbtsoc.org.uk.

Educationally disadvantaged students or students who have had a disrupted education

Oxford and Cambridge are committed to helping applicants who have in some way been disadvantaged by a poor school education or by significant disruption to their educational career, which may have resulted in candidates getting lower grades at A level than they might otherwise have achieved.

The Extenuating Circumstances Form (www.study.cam.ac.uk/under graduate/apply/ecf.html) has now replaced the Cambridge Special Access Scheme. This form enables teachers to provide detailed background information about Cambridge applicants so they can be assessed fairly. The admissions tutors will also have access to publicly available data on school performance that can help them place a student's educational achievement in context.

Cambridge advises that a school or college should submit the Extenuating Circumstances Form by the 15 October deadline if a student:

- has had a serious medical condition that caused his or her education to be upset
- is a carer
- has recently experienced a death or serious illness in his or her family.

There are four main categories of genuine Extenuating Circumstances Form applicants:

- those applicants whose backgrounds (i.e. family or school) are completely unfamiliar with the Cambridge applications process
- applicants who have been 'adversely affected by circumstances beyond their control', i.e. family difficulties, disability, ill health or schooling problems
- those applicants whose education has been negatively affected by circumstances outside their control
- students who have been in care.

Extenuating Circumstances Forms can be obtained from any college admissions office, from the University's admissions office or from the university website.

Oxford encourages teachers to include details of any special circumstances or other relevant information in their reference in the main UCAS application form. Like Cambridge, Oxford uses publicly available information to put in context those applicants who may have experienced educational or socio-economic disadvantages. Although Oxford does not have a form akin to the Extenuating Circumstances Form, it does state: 'In some circumstances candidates who miss their conditional offer may be accepted anyway if there are extenuating circumstances such as illness' (www.ox.ac.uk/about/facts-and-figures/admissions-statistics/undergraduate-admissions-statistics/qualifications).

Both universities are keen to identify bright students whatever their background. If applicants can show the necessary academic aptitude, they will probably be considered for interview and seen in addition to students identified through the standard UCAS process.

2| Money matters

This chapter will try to give you an idea of what it costs to study at Oxford or Cambridge. There is a commonly held misconception that an Oxbridge education is more expensive than other universities; however, this is not the case.

Both universities are keen to ensure that no talented student should be barred from studying with them because of the cost, and they are aware that the financial backgrounds of their applicants are varied. There are generous bursary schemes available if you are facing financial difficulty – most colleges want to take the best students regardless of income and don't want money worries distracting you from your degree.

Accommodation in both cities is expensive compared with that in other regional universities, but many colleges provide accommodation for their students for all three or four years of their courses. Oxford suggests budgeting between £4,176 and £5,304 per year for college accommodation; this would be for term time only (www.ox.ac.uk/ students/fees_funding/living_costs). Private accommodation varies, but it will be higher (www.oxfordstudentpas.co.uk/accommodation and www.admin.ox.ac.uk/accommodation/private).

At Cambridge, accommodation prices start from around £655 per month, including all bills (www.accommodation.cam.ac.uk/universityowned).

If cost is a consideration, you should ensure that the college you choose offers accommodation for the whole of your course as 'living in' is generally cheaper than 'living out'.

Living expenses are generally in line with other universities in the south of England.

The cost of studying at Oxford or Cambridge

When you are studying at any university in the UK, you will have to take into account two main types of cost: your tuition fees and your living costs. Government loans are available for all students towards both types of cost and you should contact your local student finance office to see what is on offer. You do not need to pay either for your tuition fees or for your basic term-time living costs up front. It is worth visiting the government's Student Finance website for more details: www.gov.uk/ browse/education/student-finance.

Tuition fees

Like other UK universities, the usual annual cost of tuition fees at Oxford and Cambridge for EU and UK undergraduates is £9,000. It should be borne in mind that students at Oxford and Cambridge benefit from far more teaching time and individual attention than the average student at other UK universities. For overseas students the cost of tuition fees is higher. At Oxford, the annual cost ranges between £14,845 and £21,855, and this cost is further increased for clinical medicine. At Cambridge, the annual fees range from £15,063 for the humanities, through £22,923 for engineering and science degrees, to £36,459 for medicine and veterinary science (www.gov.uk/student-finance/loans-and-grants; www.ox.ac.uk/admissions/undergraduate/fees-and-funding/tuition-fees; www.study.cam.ac.uk/undergraduates/international/finance/#tuition).

Table 2 Oxford fee reduction

Household income	Fee in first year	Fee after first year
£0–£16,000	£3,500	£6,000
£16,001–£20,000	£7,000	£7,000
£20,001–£25,000	£8,000	£8,000
£25,001+	£9,000	£9,000

Source: www.ox.ac.uk/admissions/undergraduate_courses/student_funding/2014-funding.html
Reproduced with the permission of the Chancellor, Master and Scholars of the University of Oxford.

Living costs

The UK government and universities offer financial support to help with living costs, and the level of support you receive will be dependent on your household income.

Government funding through Student Finance offers English students £3,731 as a basic maintenance loan whatever their household income. Students from households with incomes less than £42,620 will receive an additional non-repayable grant of between £3,387 and £50 depending on household income. Students from households with incomes less than £25,000 will be entitled to a full grant of £3,387. Welsh and Northern Irish students should consult their respective student finance bodies as figures may differ slightly: www.studentfinancewales.co.uk and www.studentfinanceni.co.uk.

Table 3 Estimated living costs at Oxford University

	Per month		Total for 9 months	
	Lower range	Upper range	Lower range	Upper range
Food	£260	£292	£2,337	£2,621
Accommodation (including utilities)	£460	£654	£4,138	£5,884
Personal items	£117	£239	£1,052	£2,144
Social activities	£59	£105	£528	£941
Study costs	£35	£72	£308	£648
Other	£19	£43	£193	£402
Total	£951	£1,405	£8,556	£12,641

The table range estimates are based on a single student with no dependents living in University of Oxford undergraduate college accommodation (including utility bills) in 2015–16, as of 25 November 2014. Please note that figures may be refreshed online at any time.
Reproduced with the permission of the Chancellor, Master and Scholars of the University of Oxford.

Oxford offers additional financial support to students already receiving a government grant.

Table 4 Oxford bursary support

Household income	Annual Oxford bursary
£16,000 or less	£4,500
£16,001–£20,000	£3,500
£20,001–£25,000	£5,000
£25,001–£30,000	£2,000
£30,001–£35,000	£1,500
£35,001–£40,000	£1,000
£40,001–£42,620	£500
£42,621 +	£0

Source: www.ox.ac.uk/admissions/undergraduate/fees-and-funding/oxford-support
This table shows the annual bursaries available from the University of Oxford for Home and EU students who start their first undergraduate course in 2015, dependent upon household income before tax, as assessed by the Student Loans Company. Please note that Oxford's financial support package changes annually for new entrants and is subject to approval by the Office for Fair Access each July preceding application.
Reproduced with the permission of the Chancellor, Master and Scholars of the University of Oxford.

Students from Scotland will be entitled to support for living costs. This will include a basic maintenance loan of at least £4,750 and, depending on household income, additional support in the form of an increased maintenance loan and a non-repayable Young Students' Bursary. For more details see www.saas.gov.uk.

Cambridge indicates that students should budget £8,150 a year for living costs. This includes college accommodation at £2,740–£3,600 (or £3,000–£4,200 if you are staying in en-suite accommodation), kitchen facilities at £400–£500, and college meals at £3–£4 each. As with Oxford, there are government loans available to all UK students to cover living costs, and students from lower-income households are entitled to grants.

Cambridge offers an additional scheme to students who are eligible for a government grant: the Cambridge Bursary Scheme.

> 'The Cambridge Bursary Scheme offers UK and EU students Bursaries of up to £10,500 over three years or £14,000 over four years to help them with their living costs. The value of the Bursary you receive will be dependent on your household income, with the maximum award in 2014–15 being £3,500. The Bursary can be used to help with maintenance costs or to reduce tuition fees by up to £3,000 each year.
>
> Bursaries of £3,500 a year will be available to students from families with household incomes of £25,000 or less per year. Students with household incomes of between £25,001 and £42,600 will receive a lower level Cambridge Bursary each year.
>
> A higher Bursary of £5,650 per year will be available to UK mature students with family incomes below £25,000 per year who are also resident in Cambridge throughout the year.'
>
> Source: www.study.cam.ac.uk/undergraduate/finance/
> support.html

The Cambridge Bursary Scheme also provides European bursaries to help EU students meet their living costs (www.admin.ac.uk/univ/cambridgebursary).

Practicalities

At both universities, you may prefer to make your own food rather than eat in hall all the time. Most colleges have adequate kitchen facilities and you can buy fresh food from the local markets and supermarkets quite cheaply. You will also need to budget a small amount each week to do your laundry. Most colleges have a laundry room with washing machines and tumble dryers and these cost approximately £3. Of course, this would all depend on your lifestyle.

Transport

You won't need to spend money getting around the university as both are easily navigable by bike or on foot.

If it is raining, some students prefer to take the bus to their lectures at a cost of about £1 per ride. However, most students cycle everywhere. This is by far the fastest and the cheapest way to travel. If you don't have a bike already you can pick one up from one of the many second-hand bike shops in both cities from as little as £35 (although if you want a better ride you will obviously have to pay more). Additional costs to consider when investing in a bike include: the helmet at approximately £25; locking systems to prevent theft (very important) at about £15–£20; and servicing charges. There are many bike mechanics across both cities who will fix your bike for a fee. However, college porters usually have free bike repair kits and there are normally bike reps (students whom you can call on for help with mending and servicing your wheels for absolutely no charge) at each college.

Study materials

Most books that you'll need are available in college and university libraries, so your expenses should be limited to the usual items of stationery that you had at school. Unless you're specifically instructed to buy books by your faculty, it's probably best to wait until you arrive before spending lots of money unnecessarily.

You will probably want to purchase a laptop, if you don't already own one.

Scientists may need to purchase lab coats and mathematicians may need to buy calculators. Again, you will be told by the college if you need any specific study materials for your course.

Case study: Kathy, St Edmund's Hall, Oxford

Something that some students find difficult when they go to university is that they have to manage their own finances and it can be hard to do this when you have always relied on your parents before, and when you have a limited budget. I find it very useful to keep a log of how much I am spending on things such as food, clothes and books, so that I have enough money to last me for each term. I am an international student and I spent two years in London living on my own when I was studying for my A levels, so this gave me a big advantage over some of the home students who are studying at the same college as me. My previous experience of managing a budget meant that I did not find it as difficult as some of my fellow students. In fact, I was able to offer them some advice!

I regularly cook my own food and some of my friends also cook their own food, so we can take turns eating at each other's accommodation. We buy our own ingredients and we try to do this as cheaply as possible, so this helps to keep our costs down.

I will also eat in college, things such as snacks and so on. This can be much cheaper than outside college, so again it keeps my costs down. Indeed, I try to make as much use of the college and university facilities as possible, as this way it can be cheaper than buying things outside.

I do not spend very much on socialising. I participate fully in events put on by my Chinese society, so I am still connected to lots of people, both Chinese and people from other nationalities who are interested in Chinese culture. However, even though I help to organise these events, it does not cost me very much personally to be involved in them.

As an international student, my tuition fees are more expensive and of course my travelling costs are much higher, as I try to travel back to China during my long vacations. Even so, my living costs are actually not as high as those of some of my fellow students. The important thing is to be careful about what you are spending and to keep a log of what you are spending money on.

Case study: One parent's view on the cost of studying at Oxford

My daughter Eve lived off her student loan, but she also worked during almost all of her holidays and sometimes during term time, so she did not rely on me for any financial support at all, at least not directly. Most of the people I knew with sons or daughters at university had to provide a fair bit of financial support, so I suppose I was fortunate that my daughter was so independent.

She lived cheaply while at university, taking a great deal of care about what she spent and not being extravagant. She got jobs waitressing and working in bookshops. She did not spend a great deal on books, but made maximum use of the college library, which was very well stocked. She also used the Bodleian Library regularly, as well as her faculty library. I would advise anyone with a son or daughter to pass on the tip to their children to do the same, as buying books can be expensive for students and for the parents who have to support them. This was one area in which I thought I could help: I regularly purchased books for special occasions, which my daughter could accept while still preserving her independence. I also gave a present of a laptop when my daughter was first setting off for university, which proved to be an invaluable resource.

(Eve attended Keble College, Oxford)

Scholarships, college awards and prizes

Additional sources of funding may be available from your college and you should consult individual college websites for full details. These can include:

- prizes for academic and other achievements
- grants for study-related books and equipment
- travel grants
- grants and loans to help with unforeseen financial difficulties.

There are a limited number of academic scholarships available at Oxford and Cambridge.

These include:

- Moritz-Heyman Scholarship (www.ox.ac.uk/admissions/undergraduate/fees_funding/oxford_support/moritz_heyman_scholarship)
- Oxford Centre for Islamic Studies Scholarship (www.ox.ac.uk/feesandfunding/prospectivegrad/scholarships/university/ocis)
- Palgrave Brown UK Scholarship (www.ox.ac.uk/admissions/undergraduate_courses/student_funding/palgrave_brown_uk.html)
- Lloyds Scholars Bursary (www.ox.ac.uk/admissions/undergraduate_courses/student_funding/lloyds_scholars.html).

Individual colleges may also offer scholarships and bursaries generously provided by former students. For example, a contemporary of mine at Lady Margaret Hall donated £1 million last year to the college, specifying that half would go to students who are from less privileged backgrounds, with the rest going towards his subject, PPE, and to college projects. Cambridge advises that individual colleges may have specific awards and grants, which are listed on the college websites (www.study.cam.ac.uk/undergraduate/finance/colleges/html).

Music awards and scholarships

Both universities are well known for the excellence and diversity of their music-making. One of the ways they maintain their high standards of musicianship is by offering music awards to students. Music award-holders are among the hardest-working students in the universities, as they have to juggle extensive musical commitments with their academic studies. The experience they gain is huge, though, and the opportunity to sing with, play in orchestras with or conduct some of the best young musicians in the country is unique. Many award-holders go on to careers in music.

If you're a talented musician, it is worth considering applying for a scholarship. The way you apply is different from the normal route and needs careful explanation. At both universities you can apply for organ or choral scholarships and there are some special awards for répétiteurs and chamber music.

Most colleges have open days where you can find out more about the awards and you are strongly advised to attend them to better understand the application process. You will also have the opportunity of meeting current music award-holders and visiting the colleges to see their facilities for music-making.

Auditions generally take place in September. An offer of a choral or organ scholarship does not guarantee you a place at a college as you will still need to go through the normal admissions procedure and achieve the necessary grades.

Some colleges will not allow students studying certain subjects to be music scholars because the academic demands of their courses are too great.

Anyone wishing to apply for a music award needs to read the relevant university and college websites very carefully for full details of the awards and the application process. For more information visit:

- Cambridge: www.study.cam.ac.uk/undergraduate/apply/musicawards
- Oxford: www.music.ox.ac.uk/apply/undergraduate/choral-and-organ-awards.

Choral awards

In all, 13 colleges at Oxford and 21 colleges at Cambridge offer choral awards, covering the whole range of voices: sopranos, contraltos, countertenors, tenors, baritones and basses. The basic duty of choral scholars is to sing at chapel services, but their involvement in college and university music goes further than this, extending to solo work, chamber groups and choruses. These and several of the mixed-voice choirs undertake concerts, tours and recordings, with some of these activities falling within the vacation periods. A number of colleges offer singing lessons as part of the award.

Case study: Jack, Trinity College Cambridge

Being a choral scholar is one of the best experiences that Oxbridge has to offer. It's enormously enriching musically, is masses of fun and has some amazing perks. There are also choirs for all levels of commitment and ability: John's and King's do around seven services per week, Trinity do three, while some smaller colleges only do one. Shop around to find a choir that suits you!

I'm a choral scholar at Trinity, and it has been the best part of my time at Cambridge. We sing three services and rehearse for around five hours per week. It seems a lot, but one of the best things about being a choral scholar is ... well, the other choral scholars! We're all pretty firm friends, and this makes rehearsals fly by – there are also regular pub trips, film nights etc. It's a fantastic group to be part of socially, and I'm sure all Oxbridge choirs are the same.

This is without mentioning the rest of the perks of the job: free Feasts (five-course dinners) six or seven times a year, money off our college bill each term, free singing lessons with internationally renowned teachers, lots of drinks parties hosted by our amazing Chaplains and Directors of Music, all-expenses-paid tours abroad ... (Canada last year and the USA and Australia in the next couple of years – guaranteed to be among the most fun weeks of your entire life).

If you're interested in singing and interested in being a choral scholar, then the best thing to do is to get in touch with some of the Directors of Music at Oxford or Cambridge and arrange an informal meeting. They'll be able to give you advice as to which college might be best for you, what life as a choral scholar is like, and how to balance work–life commitments while at Oxbridge. Their email addresses will be on their college's website, and they are always happy to field any queries. It's worth mentioning also that you don't have to have been a chorister/sung your whole life; the majority of choral scholars haven't, and some of Cambridge's best singers only began singing in the Sixth Form at school. Neither should you feel hidebound to apply to your own college's choir – many people sing at colleges other than their own.

For me, singing in Trinity Choir has been a real privilege. We get to work with some amazing musicians and at a really high standard while having enormous amounts of fun. Whether you are interested in singing seven services a week or one, it's a decision that you won't regret.

Organ awards

Organ scholarships are offered by 22 Oxford and 23 Cambridge colleges. The organ scholar is responsible for running the chapel music where there is no music tutor involved, and also for playing a leading part in the college's musical life in general. The experience is invaluable for musicians interested in directing and organising musical activities across a wide spectrum. Colleges normally assist in the cost of organ lessons. While researching the updates for this edition of the book, I had the pleasure of hearing the organ scholar from Sidney Sussex College, Cambridge perform in the chapel of Queen's College, Cambridge.

Répétiteur scholarships

The répétiteur scholarship is open to pianists who are interested in coaching singers. It is offered jointly by St Catherine's College, Oxford and New Chamber Opera. This offers the possibility of extensive experience as a répétiteur in the musical theatre. (www.newchamberopera. co.uk/about/repetiteur_scholarship/).

3 | Entry requirements

By now you may have decided that you'd like to apply to Oxford or Cambridge. How do you know if you're a suitable candidate and if you have a realistic chance of getting in?

It goes without saying that entry is very competitive and we've all read stories in the newspapers about students with perfect grades failing to get a place and others with lesser grades somehow being successful. It's important to understand the facts and forget the fiction.

Oxford University makes conditional offers for students studying A levels ranging between A*A*A and AAA (or 38–40 points in the International Baccalaureate including core points, or AAAAB/AAAAA in Scottish Highers, or another equivalent) depending on the subject. For humanities at Oxford the offers are generally AAA, for sciences A*AA and for mathematics A*A*A*. It has to be said that students who gain a place generally have A*A*A for the whole range of courses. Specific A level (or equivalent) subjects may be required to apply for some subjects, especially in the sciences, and some subjects require applicants to sit a written test or submit written work. (www.ox.ac.uk/admissions/undergraduate/courses/entrance-requirements/level-offers).

Cambridge colleges will require A*AA in three A level subjects (or equivalent), although they have the discretion to make non-standard offers where appropriate as part of their holistic assessment of candidates. The typical conditional A level offer for arts subjects, as well as for psychological and behavioural sciences for 2015 entry will be A*AA, while the typical offer for the other sciences will be A*A*A*. Applicants may be asked to submit written work or sit a test (i.e. the Biomedical Admissions Test (BMAT) or a college-based test). (www.study.com.ac.uk/undergraduate/apply/requirements)

Both universities interview the majority of undergraduate applicants. For some courses, for example those with fewer applicants, more than 90% of applicants are shortlisted for interview. However, for more competitive courses as few as 30% of applicants may proceed to the interview stage (www.study.cam.ac.uk/undergraduate/teachers; www.study.cam.ac.uk/undergraduate/apply/interviews).

So, here are some important questions to consider before you apply.

Are you studying the right subjects?

The AS and A level subject choices you make in Year 11 (or equivalent) can have a significant impact on the course options available to you at university.

The Russell Group, which represents the leading 24 UK universities (including Oxford and Cambridge), has produced a detailed guide to post-16 subject choices, *Informed Choices*. First published in 2011 and revised annually, this report should now be obligatory reading for every A level candidate (www.russellgroup.ac.uk/informed-choices. aspx).

Informed Choices, produced in collaboration with the Institute of Career Guidance, is aimed at all students considering A level and equivalent options. It includes advice on the best subject combinations for a wide range of university courses as well as advice on the best choices if you don't know what you want to study after school and need to keep your options open.

Informed Choices lists the so-called 'facilitating' subjects. These are the ones that the Russell Group judges to be the most effective for gaining a place at university. They are:

- mathematics and further mathematics
- English (literature)
- geography
- history
- biology
- chemistry
- physics
- languages (classical and modern).

The guide states that even where these choices are not specified as required subjects, universities may still have a preference for them.

It warns: 'If you decide not to choose some of the facilitating subjects at advanced level, many degrees at competitive universities will not be open to you.' It goes on to say that students who decide to take more than one 'soft' subject should be cautious. It suggests that the 'soft' subjects are those with a vocational or practical bent, and lists examples such as media studies, art and design, photography and business studies.

When the Oxford and Cambridge admissions tutors assess candidates, they consider not only the individual A level (or equivalent) subjects taken but also the combination of subjects. Generally they prefer applicants to have taken certain subjects or combinations of subjects which they feel will help their studies once they arrive at their universities. Recommended subjects required by Oxford and Cambridge are in accordance with the *Informed Choices* list.

Many Oxford and Cambridge courses require prior knowledge of certain subjects. If you have already decided on a course that you would like to study at university, it's recommended that you review the information given on the Oxford and Cambridge websites (www.study.cam.ac.uk/undergraduate/apply/requirements/course.html and www.ox.ac.uk/admissions/undergraduate_courses/courses/selection_criteria) before you finalise your A level subject choices, to check that they will be appropriate for an Oxbridge application. The Cambridge website specifies that there are some A levels that are useful for specific courses, some that are desirable, some that are highly desirable and some that are essential.

Some students choose to take two arts and two science subjects at AS level because they believe it will keep their options open. While such a subject combination does provide a suitable preparation for many arts and social science courses at university, you should be aware that it can make you a less competitive applicant for broad-based science courses.

Some A level subjects are considered either essential or useful for a number of courses at Oxbridge, therefore choosing one or more of these will help keep your options open.

Arts and social science courses

If you are undecided about which arts or social sciences course you'd like to study at university, then English literature, history, languages and mathematics are good 'facilitating' subjects: choosing one or more of these will provide a good foundation for your subject combination.

Other good choices to combine with these subjects include: an additional language, ancient history, classical civilisation, economics, further mathematics, geography, philosophy, religious studies and sciences (biology, chemistry or physics).

Other possible subject choices might be archaeology, citizenship, English language, environmental science, government and politics, history of art, law, music, psychology or sociology.

Science courses

If you are interested in studying a science course at university but you are not sure which one, you are advised to take at least two, and ideally three, of biology, chemistry, mathematics and physics. Some pairings of these subjects are more natural than others. The most natural pairs are biology and chemistry, chemistry and physics, and mathematics and physics.

In practice, the vast majority of applicants for science courses at Oxbridge take at least three of these subjects. Another useful combination is mathematics, further mathematics and physics. Many students take four of biology, chemistry, mathematics, further mathematics and physics.

If you are planning to study biological or medical sciences you should take chemistry; for physical sciences or engineering you should take mathematics and physics and, ideally, further mathematics.

Other possible subject choices, for instance computing, design and technology, electronics or psychology, may be useful preparation for some science courses.

Medicine

If you are considering applying for medicine at **Oxford**, you will need to achieve A*AA in three A levels including chemistry, which is compulsory, plus biology and/or physics and/or mathematics. Other academic subjects are considered acceptable, but not critical thinking or general studies.

Scottish students must have AA (including chemistry) in their Advanced Highers plus AAAAA in their Highers, which must include biology or mathematics or physics. International Baccalaureate (IB) students need a minimum total score of 38, 39 or 40 including core points depending on the course with 7, 6, 6 at Higher level. Candidates must take chemistry and a second science (biology or physics) and/or mathematics to Higher level. (www.ox.ac.uk/admissions/undergraduate/international-students/international-qualifications) If you have any concerns about what subjects are suitable, you can email Oxford at admissions@med-school.ox.ac.uk.

If biology, physics or mathematics have not been taken to A level (or equivalent), applicants must show that they have received a basic education in those subjects (achieving at least a grade C at GCSE, National 5 or Intermediate 2, or equivalent). The GCSE Double Award Combined Sciences is also acceptable. (www.ox.ac.uk/admissions/undergraduate/courses_listing/medicine).

All candidates have to take the BMAT as part of their application (see page 103 for more on this).

The **Cambridge Medicine Faculty** lists its requirements as follows: students will need a grade C or above in GCSE (or equivalent) Double Award Science and mathematics and you can substitute two single awards in GCSE biology and physics for Double Award Science. At AS or A level you need to aim for A*AA passes in chemistry and two of biology/human biology, physics and mathematics. Most applicants for medicine at Cambridge have at least three science or mathematics A levels and some colleges require this or ask for particular A level subject(s). You will need to see individual college websites for details. If you apply with only two science or mathematics subjects at A level, your likelihood of success will be reduced.

The GCSE and AS/A level subject requirements also apply to the IB. Individual Middle Years Programme subject results validated by the IB at grade 4 or above will satisfy the GCSE requirements. Standard level subjects are approximately equivalent to AS levels, and Higher level subjects are broadly comparable with A levels. Your final IB score should be 40–41 points, with 7, 7, 6 at Higher level.

Like Oxford, all medical applicants have to take the BMAT test.

You can find full details at www.study.cam.ac.uk/undergraduate/ courses/medicine.

Other A level subjects

There are other subjects not mentioned above, such as general studies and critical thinking, but Oxford and Cambridge will usually only consider these as a fourth A level subject.

Do you have the right qualifications?

There are no set 'grade requirements' for applying to Oxbridge but that doesn't mean that you don't have to be an excellent student to gain a place. Oxford and Cambridge are considered Britain's 'elite' universities; in the words of one Cambridge admissions tutor: 'We are the best university in the world and we want the best undergraduates in the world.'

There is an interactive graph generator into which prospective students can enter the name of the college to which they wish to apply and the course in order to see specific statistics on applications and acceptance rates on the Cambridge website: www.study.cam.ac.uk/ undergraduate/apply/statistics. The figures for Oxford can be found on: www.ox.ac.uk/about/facts-and-figures/admissions-statistics.

You will need consistently high grades, a glowing reference from your current school or college, and to be able to demonstrate commitment to your chosen course in your personal statement and interview. Each year, thousands of students apply for a place at both universities; for instance, over 17,400 undergraduate applications were made to

Oxford for 2013 entry and over 16,100 applied to Cambridge, with the success rate for Oxford standing at 20.1% and that of Cambridge at 20.8%. However, this should not put you off trying if you fulfil the universities' basic requirements. Remember, someone has to get in and not everyone who applies is a genius. To state the obvious: if you don't apply, you won't get in!

Set out below is information given by the Oxford and Cambridge websites regarding their requirements for an offer of a place.

Cambridge requirements in detail

Although the website mainly talks in terms of GCSEs and A levels, other school and national examinations at an equivalent level are equally acceptable. Whatever system you're being educated in, Cambridge requires top grades in the highest-level qualifications available for school students. Most of the information below has been taken from the Cambridge admissions website (www.cam.ac.uk/admissions/undergraduate).

If you are taking any other examination system (including the Advanced International Certificate of Education offered by Cambridge Assessment), it is a good idea to make early contact with the Cambridge admissions office to check that it provides an appropriate preparation for the course you hope to study.

Much of what is stated in the following pages can of course also be found on the Cambridge website and it is always advisable to check the website in case there have been any changes since the publication of this book.

AS levels

If you are applying to Cambridge you should usually study four subjects, although it is not unheard of for students to study five. However, taking four subjects does not put you at a disadvantage to those students taking five. You do not have to cash in your AS levels, but the Supplementary Application Questionnaire requires you to put down the results of all AS and A level examinations taken. You will not get a conditional offer based solely on your AS grades.

A levels

While most applicants to Cambridge are taking three or four A level subjects, the usual conditional A level offer for entry in 2015 is A*AA.

The subject in which the A* is to be achieved is unlikely to be specified in most cases. As mentioned already, the usual conditional A level offer for arts subjects and for psychological and behavioural sciences for 2015 entry will be A*AA, while the usual conditional offer for the other sciences will be A*A*A*.

Colleges may alter offers depending on an individual's case. For instance, mitigating circumstances may be taken into account if an Extenuating Circumstances Form has been completed; conversely, higher offers may be made if there is some doubt about a student's potential.

Extended project

The extended project (EP) is taken by some students in addition to their A levels, which focuses on planning, research and evaluative skills, skills which are valued by higher education bodies such as Cambridge as well as by future employers. Although neither Oxford nor Cambridge will use the EP in its offers, Cambridge has stated that the EP may be used for discussion at interview and it may even form the basis of written work, in some circumstances. Cambridge further states that it welcomes the EP as it helps to develop independent study and the research skills valued in higher education.

AQA Baccalaureate

The AQA Baccalaureate may be used as an entry qualification for Cambridge, but offers are dependent of the results of individual A levels within the qualification rather than the whole award.

Cambridge Pre-U

Both Oxford and Cambridge take the Pre-U into account as a qualification, but they do not prefer it above other qualifications. They value the skills it inculcates, such as independent research skills, as well as the promotion of critical, lateral and contextual thinking.

Cambridge Pre-U students, as well as students who are studying a combination of pre-U and A levels, may apply to Cambridge. Students are given conditional offers usually dependent on their achieving distinctions in their main subjects.

International Baccalaureate diploma programme

Conditional offers are frequently made on the International Baccalaureate, with scores between 40 and 41 points out of 45, with 7, 7, 6 in the Higher level subjects being required. Students should look on the Cambridge website for precise requirements and the best IB subject combinations. It should be borne in mind that Standard level subjects are comparable to AS levels, while Higher level subjects are akin to A2.

Scottish Highers and Advanced Highers

Cambridge will usually require Scottish applicants to have gained at least four A grades at Higher grade, plus Advanced Highers. Conditional offers are normally made on the basis of AAA in three Advanced Highers. Two Advanced Highers and an additional Higher may be allowed in certain circumstances. For further details, candidates are advised to peruse the Cambridge website. It should be borne in mind that Highers are roughly the same as AS level, while Advanced Highers are comparable to A2.

Applicants who are studying for the Scottish Baccalaureate will usually be required to get three Advanced Highers.

If applicants cannot study more than two Advanced Highers through no fault of their own, they should consult the colleges to which they are thinking of applying.

Welsh Baccalaureate

Students on the Advanced Diploma in the Welsh Baccalaureate should normally be taking three subjects at A level as part of their qualification. Conditional offers will be made on the basis of how well they are likely to do in the individual A levels rather than on the overall award.

Irish Leaving Certificate

Republic of Ireland applicants who are taking the Irish Leaving Certificate may apply. The usual offer for the Irish Leaving Certificate is AAAAA at Higher level.

Applicants for medicine and veterinary medicine may also be required to take an IGCSE or equivalent in the science subject which they have not covered as part of the Irish Leaving Certificate.

Access to HE Diploma

Cambridge applicants on the Access to HE (Higher Education) Diploma are normally required to reach a standard akin to conditional A level offers. As a consequence the usual offer will be distinctions in all of the requisite subject units within the Access to HE Diploma.

Applicants may also be required to meet certain subject-specific requirements; for example, an extra A level in Mathematics or evidence of proficiency in languages may be required. A list of extra requirements for each subject can be found at: www.study.cam.ac.uk/undergraduate/apply/requirements.

European Baccalaureate

Successful applicants on the European Baccalaureate are usually required to attain 85–90% overall, with 90% in the areas in closest proximity to the course they are applying to read at Cambridge.

French Baccalaureate

Applicants studying for the French Baccalaureate (including the International option) are usually required to achieve 16 or 17 ('mention très bien') out of 20. In addition, such applicants are normally required to attain 16 or 17 in specified subjects.

German Abitur

German Abitur applicants are usually required to gain an overall score of between 1.0 and 1.3, with 14 or 15 in the subjects in closest proximity to the course they are applying to read at Cambridge.

SATs and Advanced Placement Tests

If you are from the USA or Canada and you are preparing for Advanced Placement Tests or SATs, you may be considered but on a case-by-case basis. You will usually need to have done very well in your High School Diploma and the SAT, as well as having gained grade 5 in a minimum of five Advanced Placement Tests in relevant subjects.

Diplomas

Advanced Diplomas in Engineering, Manufacturing and Product Design, and Environmental and Land-based Studies are considered for entry as they are viewed as preparing candidates satisfactorily for some courses at Cambridge.

- You can apply for engineering at Cambridge with Advanced Diplomas in Engineering and in Manufacturing and Product Design on the condition that you have taken certain options from the Additional Specialist Learning component.
- You can apply for geography, land economy and natural sciences (biological) with the Advanced Diploma in Environmental and Land-based Studies on the condition that you have taken the relevant subjects in the Additional Specialist Learning component. For natural sciences (biological), these must be A level Chemistry and one of Biology, Mathematics or Physics A level. The geography and land economy requirements are more open.

VCE and Applied A Levels, GNVQs and BTECs

Vocational qualifications are not a recommended entry route to Cambridge, because of the focus on vocational rather than academic. That being said, if preferred subjects at A level have been covered, applicants may take a six-unit VCE or applied A level in lieu of a third A level or as a fourth subject to demonstrate breadth of learning. It is always worth checking with the college admissions tutor about what is acceptable, as indeed it is if you are taking any of the non-standard offers from this section.

Oxford requirements in detail

- Many students who apply to Oxford are taking A levels but any candidate who has already taken, or who is currently studying, any other equivalent qualifications is also most welcome to apply.
- Oxford will assess a student's application on their ability, regardless of their age, and it stresses that no special consideration is given to younger candidates.
- The information below outlines the general entrance requirements. The Oxford website should also be consulted: www.ox.ac.uk/admissions/undergraduate/courses/entrance-requirements.

A levels

Conditional offers of between A*A*A and AAA (depending on the subject) are made to Oxford applicants. General studies is ruled out as an approved A level, but Oxford admissions officers say that almost any other subject may be considered, on the proviso that you meet the requirements laid out by the colleges. AS scores and other unit scores are not needed for the UCAS application and they make their offers based on your final A level grades.

Extended projects

While Oxford sees the merit of the EP for the skills it develops, it will not make any offers based on it. However, if you have gained skills and experience from working on an EP, it is always worth discussing this in your personal statement.

14–19 diplomas

- While the Advanced Diploma in Engineering (Level 3) may be accepted as an entry qualification for engineering science courses at Oxford, applicants have to attain an A level in Physics and the new Level 3 Certificate in Mathematics for Engineering in addition.
- Diplomas in other subjects may be considered as acceptable entry qualifications as long as applicants have chosen Additional Specialist Learning in two appropriate A levels.

Pre-U

The Pre-U diploma is deemed to be an acceptable entry qualification. It depends on the subject, but if you are made an offer it is likely to be in the following range: D2, D2, D3 and D3, D3, D3. If in doubt, you should check the precise requirements with the faculty to which you are applying. Oxford says that D2 is regarded as similar to an A* grade at A level and D3 to an A grade. It also says that applicants may study Pre-U principal subjects instead of A levels.

Young Applicants in Schools Scheme (YASS)

Oxford welcomes applicants who have studied YASS modules. These modules are taught by the Open University, and Oxford says that they may prepare students appropriately for higher education. YASS students are advised to discuss what they have gained from their study of these modules in their personal statements, but it is likely that offers will still be made on the basis of A levels or similar qualifications, as most YASS students will also be taking these.

For students taking only Open University qualifications, an application may still be considered. Strong candidates should have achieved a minimum of 120 points at level 1, in relevant subjects.

English Baccalaureate

This has had little impact at present. It should be noted that it is more important to have achieved a strong set of GCSE grades at A and A*.

Vocational qualifications

While Oxford is happy to receive applications from students with vocational qualifications which are similar in standard to A levels, such students may also be asked for extra academic qualifications in order to reach the standards set by the admissions officers.

International Baccalaureate

International Baccalaureate students typically receive offers of 38–40 points, including core points; in addition, they need to attain 6s and 7s in the Higher level.

Scottish qualifications

At the moment, the typical offer is AAAAB or AAAAA in Scottish Highers with the addition of two or more Advanced Highers. AAB is normally required if a student is in a position to study three Advanced Highers; if a student is not able to do this, he or she would normally be required to achieve AA in two Advanced Highers, as well as an A grade in a third Higher course studied in the sixth year.

American qualifications

Oxford typically requires minimum SAT Reasoning Test scores of 700 in critical reading, mathematics and the writing paper, or ACT with a minimum score of 32 out of 36. Grade 5 in three or more Advanced Placement Tests is also required in appropriate subjects or SAT Subject Tests in three subjects with a score of 700 or more.

Other international qualifications

For more detailed information on this, please see Chapter 10, which deals with non-standard applications.

4 | The early stages of preparation

Choosing the right course is the most important decision you will have to make during the whole application process. It is primarily your enthusiasm for your subject that will be attractive to the admissions tutors and interviewers and, if you are accepted, your love for your subject will sustain you through all the hard work you will undoubtedly have to do. When considering which course to take and when preparing for interview, reading is another, and absolutely essential, form of preparation. You need to read widely and in depth. Knowing the school syllabus is not enough. You should be able to think and talk about ideas beyond the scope of school work and above the level of your peers.

The importance of reading

Remember that the academics who teach at Oxford and Cambridge, and who interview prospective students, have dedicated their whole lives to their subject. They believe passionately in the importance of their research and expect you to do the same. If you have read around your subject this shows that you are dedicated and passionate and this will be very attractive to interviewers.

In addition, if you are accepted, the majority of your time as an undergraduate will be spent working. Whereas students on an essay-based course at UCL, for example, will be asked to write four 2,500-word essays over the course of a 10-week term, Oxbridge students are asked to write between 12 and 14 essays of the same length in the course of an eight-week term. Students who study science subjects at Oxbridge will have a large amount of contact time per week. These hours are made up of lab sessions, supervisions or tutorials, seminars and lectures that fill up most of the week and may run into your weekends. There is little time off, and most of it is taken up studying for assignments and essays. You need to be excited by this work and find the pressure enjoyable rather than a burden.

The method of working at Oxbridge is very different from school. Students who study humanities subjects (English literature, history and languages, for example) typically have very few hours of contact time in the week; perhaps six to eight hours of lectures and one hour-long seminar per week. However, they are expected to work as many hours as the scientists. This requires them to be independent in their study practice. Humanities students need to be dedicated, focused and able to follow through their own research without getting distracted. Like the scientists, therefore, humanities students need to show that they are able to research independently.

Finally, in order to make the right choice, it is important to gather as much information about a course and its content as possible. Prospectuses for Oxford and Cambridge give detailed course guides, including information on course content and A level requirements. In addition, Oxford makes individual prospectuses for each subject. Read this information and the criteria very carefully, making sure your qualifications fulfil the requirements specified.

If you want to be really thorough, contact the individual faculty secretaries at the university. Remember that, while the college administers the teaching, it is the faculty (i.e. the subject department within the university) that controls the syllabus. The faculty secretary will have much more detail on course content than is available in the prospectuses. Information about faculty addresses, including website addresses, is available in the prospectuses.

When you talk with the faculty secretary, ask him or her for an up-to-date reading list for new undergraduates. This will list the books that students are expected to read before they come up to Cambridge or Oxford for the first time. If you dip into some of these books you will get an idea of the sort of information you will be tackling if you study the subject. In addition, if you have time to visit Cambridge or Oxford again, you could spend the afternoon in the university bookshop (Blackwell's in Oxford or Heffers in Cambridge). The staff at both bookshops will be very familiar with the texts used by undergraduates. Of course, if you know any current undergraduates at either university, discuss their work with them. It might also be an idea to read books on your subject from the Oxford University Press's *Very Short Introduction* series, which usually give a good overview. The *London Review of Books* is also a good source.

Collecting this information will boost your confidence and reassure you about your subject decision. Remember, in order to argue your case at interview, and to cope with the workload if you get a place, you must be deeply committed to your subject.

Recommended reading

On the following pages is a list of suggested books and films that may help you to start your research. This list is not definitive and not officially endorsed by the Oxbridge faculties. As already stated, most faculties will have a recommended reading list on their websites and you should be familiar with this.

If you need further ideas, consult the list below. Don't feel you must read every book on this list either. Dip into one or two to start with and see what particularly interests you. If your subject is not included here, or if you want to find out more, ask your teacher at your school or college for further guidance.

Archaeology and anthropology

Social anthropology

- Fox, K., *Watching the English*, Hodder & Stoughton, 2007.
- Monaghan, J. and Just, P., *Social and Cultural Anthropology: A Very Short Introduction*, OUP, 2000.

Biological anthropology

- Clack, T., *Ancestral Roots: Modern Living and Human Evolution*, Palgrave Macmillan, 2008.
- Lewin, R., *Human Evolution: An Illustrated Introduction*, Blackwell, 2005.

Archaeology

- Gamble, C., *Archaeology: The Basics*, Routledge, 2000.
- Renfrew, C. and Bahn, P., *Archaeology: Theories, Methods and Practice*, Thames & Hudson, 2008.

General books

- Barley, N., *The Innocent Anthropologist: Notes from a Mud Hut*, Waveland, 2000.
- Carrithers, M., *Why Human Beings Have Cultures*, OUP, 1992.
- Dunbar, R., *Gossip, Grooming and the Evolution of Language*, Faber, 1996.
- Fagan, B., *People of the Earth: An Introduction to World Prehistory*, Longman, 2004.
- Gosden, C., *Anthropology and Archaeology: A Changing Relationship*, Routledge, 1999.
- Harrison, G.A., *Human Biology: An Introduction to Human Evolution, Variation, Growth, and Adaptability*, OUP, 1992.
- Haviland, W., *Cultural Anthropology*, Harcourt Brace, 2003.
- Hendry, J., *An Introduction to Social Anthropology: Other People's Worlds*, Macmillan, 1999.
- Keesing, R. and Strathern, A., *Cultural Anthropology: A Contemporary Perspective*, Harcourt Brace, 1998.
- Kuper, A., *The Chosen Primate: Human Nature and Cultural Diversity*, Harvard University Press, 1996.
- Layton, R., *An Introduction to Theory in Anthropology*, CUP, 1998.

Architecture

Also look at the reading list for art history.

- Curtis, W., *Modern Architecture Since 1900*, Phaidon, 1982.
- Frampton, K., *Modern Architecture: A Critical History*, Thames & Hudson, 2007.
- Kostoff, S., *A History of Architecture, Settings and Rituals*, OUP, 1995.
- Le Corbusier, *Towards a New Architecture*, Architectural Press, 1946.
- Vitruvius, *The Ten Books on Architecture*.
- Watkin, D., *The History of Western Architecture*, Laurence King, 2011.

Art history

- Arnason, H.H. and Kalb, P., *History of Modern Art* (5th edition), Pearson, 2002.
- Baxandall, M., *Painting and Experience in Fifteenth Century Italy: A Primer in the Social History of Pictorial Style*, OUP, 1988.
- Beard, M. and Henderson, J., *Classical Art: From Greece to Rome*, OUP, 2001.
- Berger, J., *Ways of Seeing*, Penguin,1972.
- Boardman, J., ed., *Oxford History of Classical Art*, OUP, 1993.
- Camille, M., *Gothic Art: Glorious Visions*, Pearson, 1996.
- Campbell, S.J. and Cole, M.W., *A New History of Italian Renaissance Art*, Thames & Hudson, 2012.
- Clunas, C., *Art in China* (2nd edition), OUP, 2009.
- Crow, T., *The Rise of the Sixties: American and European Art in the Era of Dissent*, Laurence King, 1996.
- Elsner, J., *Imperial Art and Christian Triumph: The Art of the Roman Empire, 100–450*, OUP, 1998.
- Gombrich, E.H., *The Story of Art*, Phaidon, 1995.
- Gombrich, E.H., *Art and Illusion: A Study in the Psychology of Pictorial Representation*, Phaidon, 2002
- Greenhalgh, M., *The Classical Tradition in Art*, Duckworth, 1978.
- Harbison, C., *The Mirror of the Artist: Northern Renaissance Art in its Historical Context*, Pearson, 1995.
- Haskell, F., *History and its Images: Art and the Interpretation of the Past*, Yale University Press, 1993.
- Hockney, D., *Secret Techniques: Rediscovering the Lost Techniques of the Old Masters*, Thames & Hudson, 2006.
- Honour, H. and Fleming, J., *A World History of Art* (7th edition), Laurence King, 2005.
- Johnson, G.A., *Renaissance Art: A Very Short Introduction*, OUP, 2002.

- Kemp, M., *Behind the Picture: Art and Evidence in the Italian Renaissance*, Yale University Press, 1997.
- Kemp, M., *The Science of Art: Optical Themes in Western Art from Brunelleschi to Seurat*, Yale University Press, 1992.
- Nochlin, L., *Women, Art and Power and Other Essays*, Thames & Hudson, 1989.
- Pollitt, J.J., *Art and Experience in Classical Greece*, CUP, 1972.
- Wölfflin, H., *Principles of Art History*, Dover, 1986.

Another useful resource is BBC Four, which broadcasts a wide range of high-quality and engaging documentaries that provide a useful background for the aspiring Art historian, such as 'The Art of China' by Andrew Graham Dixon, 'The History of Art in Three Colours' by Dr James Fox and 'The Power of Art' by Simon Schama.

Biological sciences (Oxford)

- Aydon, C., *Charles Darwin: His Life and Times*, Robinson, 2008.
- Burton, R., *Biology by Numbers: An Encouragement to Quantitative Thinking*, CUP, 1998.
- Chalmers, A.F., *What is This Thing Called Science?*, Open University Press, 1998.
- Collins, H.M. and Pinch, T., *The Golem: What You Should Know About Science* (2nd edition), CUP, 1998.
- Coyne, J., *Why Evolution is True*, OUP, 2009.
- Dawkins, R., *The Selfish Gene*, OUP, 1976.
- Freedman, D., Pisani, R. and Purves, R., *Statistics* (3rd edition although any edition would do), W.W. Norton and Company, 1997.
- Gould, Stephen Jay, *The Burgess Shale and the Nature of History*, W.W. Norton and Co, 1989.
- Gribbin, J., *Science: A History, 1543–2001*, Penguin, 2002.
- Jones, S., *Almost Like a Whale*, Black Swan, 2001.
- Southwood, R., *The Story of Life*, OUP, 2003.
- Wood, B., *Human Evolution: A Very Short Introduction*, OUP, 2005.

Biochemistry (Oxford)

- Alberts, B. et al., *Molecular Biology of the Cell* (5th edition), Taylor & Francis, 2008.
- Alberts, B. et al., *Essential Cell Biology* (2nd edition), Taylor & Francis, 2003.
- Campbell, M. and Farrell, S., *Biochemistry* (6th edition), Cengage Learning, 2008.
- Devlin, T., *Textbook of Biochemistry with Clinical Correlation* (6th edition), Wiley-Liss, 2005.
- Elliott, W. and Elliott, D., *Biochemistry and Molecular Biology* (3rd edition), OUP, 2004.

- Fox, M. and Whitesell, J., *Organic Chemistry* (3rd edition), Jones & Bartlett, 2004.
- Garret, R. and Grisham, C., *Biochemistry* (3rd edition), Cengage Learning, 2005.
- Lewin, B. et al., eds, *Cells* (1st edition), Jones & Bartlett, 2007.
- Lodish et al., *Molecular Cell Biology* (6th edition), W.H. Freeman.
- Stryer et al., *Biochemistry* (6th edition), W.H. Freeman, 2004.
- Sykes, P., *Guidebook to Mechanism in Organic Chemistry* (6th edition), Prentice Hall, 1986.
- Voet, D., Voet, J. and Pratt, C., *Fundamentals of Biochemistry* (3rd edition), Wiley, 2008.

Chemistry

- Atkins, P. and de Paula, J., *Atkins' Physical Chemistry* (9th edition), OUP, 2010.
- Cotton, F.A. and Wilkinson, G., *Advanced Inorganic Chemistry* (5th edition), Wiley, 1999.
- Emsley, J., *Molecules at an Exhibition: Portraits of Intriguing Materials in Everyday Life*, OUP, 1998.
- Keeler, J. and Wothers, P., *Why Chemical Reactions Happen*, OUP, 2003.
- Morrison, R.T. and Boyd, R.N., *Organic Chemistry* (6th edition), Prentice Hall, 1992.

Chemical engineering

- Azapagic, A. et al., *Sustainable Development in Practice: Case Studies for Engineers and Scientists*, Wiley, 2004.
- Duncan, T.M. and Reimer, J.A., *Chemical Engineering Design and Analysis: An Introduction*, CUP, 1998.
- Felder, R.M. and Rousseau, R.W., *Elementary Principles of Chemical Processes*, Wiley, 2003.
- Field, R., *Chemical Engineering: Introductory Aspects*, Palgrave Macmillan, 1988.
- Freshwater, D., *People, Pipes and Processes*, IChemE, 1998.
- Solen, K.A. and Harb, J.N., *Introduction to Chemical Engineering*, Wiley, 2010.

Classics

- Davies, J.K., *Democracy and Classical Greece* (2nd edition), Fontana, 1993.
- Eliot, T.S., *The Waste Land*, Faber and Faber, 1921.
- Goodman, M., *The Roman World 44 BC – AD 180*, Routledge, 1997.
- Graves, R., *The Greek Myths*, Penguin, 2000.
- Herodotus, *The Histories*, Penguin Classics, 2003.
- Homer, *The Iliad*, Penguin Classics, 2003.
- Homer, *The Odyssey*, Penguin Classics, 2003.

- Irwin, T., *Classical Thought*, OUP, 1989.
- Parker, R., *On Greek Religion*, Cornell University Press, 2013.
- Ste Croix, G.E.M. de, *Class Struggle in the Ancient Greek World*, Duckworth 1982.
- Scullard, H.H., *From the Gracchi to Nero: a History of Rome from 133 BC to AD 68*, Routledge, 2010.
- Sophocles, *The Three Theban Plays*, Penguin, 2000.
- Thucydides, *History of the Peloponnesian War*, Penguin Classics, 2000.

Economics

- Chang, H., *Economics: The User's Guide*, Pelican Books, 2014.
- Dasgupta, P., *Economics: A Very Short Introduction*, OUP, 2007
- Jacques, I., *Mathematics for Economics and Business*, Pearson, 2012.
- Piketty, T., *Capital in the 21st Century*, Belknap Press, 2014.
- *The Economist* (weekly).
- *Financial Times* (daily).

Microeconomics

- Begg, D.K.H., Fischer, S. and Dornbusch, R., *Economics* (latest edition), McGraw-Hill.
- Dixit, A. and Skeath, S., *Games of Strategy* (2nd edition), Norton, 2009.
- Morgan, W., Katz, M. and Rosen, S., *Microeconomics* (latest edition), McGraw-Hill.
- Varian, H., *Intermediate Microeconomics* (latest edition), Norton.

Macroeconomics

- Heilbroner, R., *The Worldly Philosophers* (latest edition), Penguin.
- Mankiw, N.G. and Taylor, M.P., *Macroeconomics* (European edition), W.H. Freeman, 2007.

Quantitative methods in economics

- Aczel, A.D. and Sounderpandian, J., *Complete Business Statistics* (latest edition), McGraw-Hill/Irwin.
- Bradley, T. and Patton, P., *Essential Mathematics for Economics and Business* (latest edition), Wiley.
- Lind, D., Marchal, W. and Mason, R., *Statistical Techniques in Business and Economics* (latest edition), McGraw-Hill/Irwin.
- Pemberton, M. and Rau, N., *Mathematics for Economists* (2nd edition), Manchester University Press, 2006.

Political and sociological aspects of economics

- Donkin, R., *Blood, Sweat and Tears: The Evolution of Work*, Texere, 2001.

- Dunleavy, P. et al., *Developments in British Politics* (latest edition), Macmillan.
- Easterlin, R., *The Reluctant Economist*, CUP, 2004.
- Hutton, W., *The Writing on the Wall: China and the West in the 21st Century*, Abacus, 2007.
- Toynbee, P., *Hard Work*, Bloomsbury, 2003.

British economic history

- Broadberry, S. and Solomou, S., *Protectionism and Economic Revival: The British Inter-war Economy*, CUP, 2008.
- Floud, R. and Johnson, P., eds, *The Cambridge Economic History of Modern Britain* (three vols), CUP, 2004.
- Hudson, P., *The Industrial Revolution*, Hodder, 1992.
- Mathias, P., *The First Industrial Nation*, Routledge, 2001.

UK, European and world history

- Clarke, P., *Hope and Glory*, Penguin, 2004.
- Diamond, J., *Guns, Germs and Steel*, Vintage, 2005.
- Hobsbawm, E., *Age of Extremes: The Short Twentieth Century 1914–1991*, Abacus, 1995.
- Johnston, R. et al., eds, *The Dictionary of Human Geography* (4th edition), Blackwell, 2000.
- Judt, T., *Postwar*, Vintage, 2010.
- Landes, D.S., *The Wealth and Poverty of Nations: Why Are Some So Rich and Others So Poor?*, Norton, 1999.
- Mazower, M., *Dark Continent: Europe's Twentieth Century*, Penguin, 2008.
- Thomas, D. and Goudie, A., eds, *The Dictionary of Physical Geography* (3rd edition), Blackwell, 2000.

English

Your personal statement should identify your knowledge and appreciation of authors outside those of the English A level syllabus. It is sensible also to display an interest in different genres and periods; a student who only referred to twentieth century American literary texts would not be overly impressive. You should not simply be reeling names off but explaining why your chosen authors mean so much to you. Also, if you display an interest in the work of an author it is only sensible to have read more than one work by him or her and to have considered the cultural context in which he or she wrote.

- Barry, P., *Beginning Theory: An Introduction to Literary and Cultural Theory*, Manchester University Press, 2009.
- Bate, J., *The Soul of the Age: Life, Mind and World of William Shakespeare*, Viking, 2008.
- Culler, J., *Literary Theory: A Very Short Introduction*, OUP, 2011.

- Culler, J., *On Deconstruction: Theory and Criticism after Structuralism*, Routledge, 2008.
- Culler, J., *Structuralist Poetics*, Routledge, 2002.
- Daiches, D., *Critical Approaches to English Literature*, Kessinger, 2007.
- Eagleton, T., *Literary Theory: An Introduction*, University of Minnesota Press, 1983.
- Eagleton, T., *The English Novel: An Introduction*, Blackwell Publishing, 2005.
- Guerin, W.L. et al., *A Handbook of Approaches to Literature*, OUP, 2010.
- Hopkins, C., *Thinking About Texts: An Introduction to English Studies*, Palgrave Macmillan, 2009.
- Kerrigan, J., *Revenge Tragedy: From Aeschylus to Armageddon*, Clarendon Press, 1997.
- *Norton Anthology of Poetry, The*, W.W. Norton & Co, 2005.
- Nuttall, A.D., *Why Does Tragedy Give Pleasure?*, OUP, 2001.
- Nuttall, A.D., *A New Mimesis*, Methuen, 1983.
- Young, T., *Studying English Literature. A Practical Guide*, CUP, 2008.

History

The key piece of advice for would-be Oxbridge historians is to ensure that you have read widely around your A level topics. You need to show an awareness of recent historical debate and to understand different interpretations of the same events. The books listed below either deal with historiography or are particularly well written and deserve attention.

- Bartlett, R., *The Making of Europe: Conquest, Colonization and Cultural Change, 950–1350*, Penguin, 1994.
- Blanning, T., *Pursuit of Glory: Europe 1648–1815*, Penguin, 2008.
- Burleigh, M., *Earthly Powers*, Harper Perennial, 2006.
- Cannadine, D., *In Churchill's Shadow*, Penguin, 2003.
- Davies, C.S.L., *Peace, Print and Protestantism 1450–1558*, Paladin, 1977.
- Elton, G., *The Practice of History*, Wiley-Blackwell, 2001.
- Evans, R.J., *In Defence of History*, Granta, 2001.
- Ferguson, N., *Civilization*, Penguin, 2011.
- Hobsbawm, E., Ranger, T., (eds), *The Invention of Tradition*, Cambridge University Press, 1983.
- Hobsbawm, E., *On History*, Weidenfeld and Nicolson, 1997.
- Judt, T., *Postwar: A History of Europe since 1945*, Vintage, 2010.
- Mazower, M., *Dark Continent: Europe's Twentieth Century*, Penguin, 1999.

- Nasar, S., *Grand Pursuit: The Story of the People who Made Modern Economics*, Fourth Estate, 2012.
- Pagden, A., *The Enlightenment and Why it Still Matters*, OUP, 2013.
- Worden, B., *Roundhead Reputations*, Penguin, 2002.

Students would also be advised to search out relevant articles in the *London Review of Books*, *Literary Review* and *History Today*.

Law

- Appleton, C., *Life after Life Imprisonment*, OUP, 2010.
- Berlins, M. and Dyer, C., *The Law Machine*, Penguin, 2000.
- Lord Denning, *The Discipline of Law*, OUP, 1979.
- De Schutter, O., *International Human Rights Law: Cases, Materials, Commentary*, CUP, 2010.
- Griffith, J.A.G., *The Politics of the Judiciary*, Fontana, 2010.
- Grove, T., *The Juryman's Tale*, Bloomsbury, 2000.
- Grove, T., *The Magistrate's Tale*, Bloomsbury, 2003.
- Holland, J.A. and Webb, J.S., *Learning Legal Rules*, OUP, 2010.
- Klarman, M.J., *Brown v. Board of Education and the Civil Rights Movement*, OUP, 2007.
- McBride, N., *Letters to a Law Student*, Longman, 2010.
- McLeod, I., *Legal Method*, Palgrave Macmillan, 2011.
- Pritchard, J., *The New Penguin Guide to the Law*, Penguin, 2004.
- Shaw, M, *International Law*, CUP, 2008.
- Smith, A.T.H., *Glanville Williams: Learning the Law*, Sweet & Maxwell, 2010. (This is a popular introductory book. It will not give you any specific, substantive legal knowledge, but it will provide you with useful information ranging from how to read cases to what the abbreviations mean.)
- Vidal, J., *McLibel: Burger Culture on Trial*, Pan Books, 1997.
- Waldron, J., *The Law*, Routledge, 1990.

Linguistics

- Akmajian, A., *Linguistics: An Introduction to Language and Communication*, MIT Press, 2001.
- Atkinson, M. et al., *Foundations of General Linguistics*, Unwin Hyman, 1988.
- Fromkin, V. et al., *An Introduction to Language*, Thomson/Heinle, 2003.
- Murray, N., *Writing Essays in English Language and Linguistics: Principles, Tips and Strategies for Undergraduates*, CUP, 2012.
- Newmeyer, F.J., ed., *Linguistics: The Cambridge Survey*, CUP, 1998.
- Pinker, S., *The Language Instinct*, William Morrow and Company, 1994.
- Radford, A., *Linguistics: An Introduction*, CUP, 1999.

Management

- Dixit, A. and Nalebuff, B., *Thinking Strategically: The Competitive Edge in Business, Politics, and Everyday Life*, W.W. Norton and Co., 1991.
- Handy, C., *Understanding Organisations* (4th edition), Penguin, 1993.
- McCraw, T.K., *Creating Modern Capitalism: How Entrepreneurs, Companies, and Countries Triumphed in Three Industrial Revolutions*, Harvard Business School Press, 1998.
- Pfeffer, J., *The Human Equation: Building Profits by Putting People First*, Harvard Business School Press, 1998.
- Pfeffer, J. and Sutton, R., *Hard Facts, Dangerous Half-Truths and Total Nonsense: Profiting from Evidence-Based Management*, Harvard Business School Press, 2006.
- Tedlow, R., *New and Improved: The Story of Mass Marketing in America*, McGraw-Hill, 1996.

Medicine

- Asimov, I., *New Guide to Science*, Penguin, 1993.
- Bryson, B., *A Short History of Nearly Everything*, Black Swan, 2004.
- Calvin, W.H. and Ojemann, G., *Conversations with Neil's Brain*, Basic Books, 1995.
- Greenfield, S., *The Human Brain: A Guided Tour*, Weidenfeld & Nicolson, 1997.
- Goldacre, B, *Bad Science*, Fourth Estate, 2008.
- Goldacre, B, *Bad Pharma*, Fourth Estate, 2012.
- Jeffreys, D., *Aspirin*, Bloomsbury, 2005.
- Konner, Dr M., *The Trouble with Medicine*, BBC Books, 1993.
- Medawar, P.B., *Advice to a Young Scientist*, Basic Books, 1981.
- Noble, D., *The Music of Life: Biology Beyond Genes*, OUP, 2008.
- Nuland, S., *How We Die*, Vintage, 1997.
- Nuland, S., *How We Live*, Vintage, 1998.
- Revill, J., *Everything You Need to Know about Bird Flu*, Rodale, 2005.
- Ridley, M., *Genome*, Fourth Estate, 2000.
- Sacks, O., *The Man Who Mistook His Wife for a Hat*, Picador, 2011.
- Seedhouse, D. and Lovett, L., *Practical Medical Ethics*, Wiley-Blackwell, 1992.
- Thomas, L., *The Youngest Science*, Penguin, 1995.
- Watson, J., *DNA: The Secret of Life*, Arrow, 2004.
- Weatherall, D.J., *Science and the Quiet Art*, W.W. Norton & Co., 1995.
- Wilham, Dr D., *Body Story*, Channel 4 Books, 1998.

Modern languages

French: reading

- Albert Camus, *La Chute*.
- Marie Cardinal, *La Clé sur la Porte*.
- Gustave Flaubert, *Trois Contes*.
- André Gide, *La Porte étroite*.
- Victor Hugo, *Le Dernier jour d'un condamné*.
- Molière, *Le Misanthrope*.
- Marcel Proust, *Du Côté de chez Swann*.
- La Rochefoucauld, *Maximes*.
- Voltaire, *Candide* or *Micromegas* (short story).

French: films

François Truffaut, Robert Bresson, André Téchiné, Eric Rohmer and Louis Malle are important figures in French cinema. Read the following texts if possible:

- Bresson, *Notes Sur le Cinématographe*.
- Truffaut, *Les Films de Ma Vie*.

German: reading

- Heinrich Böll, *Die verlorene Ehre der Katharina Blum*.
- Bertolt Brecht, *Der kaukasischer Kreidekreis*; *Mutter Courage*.
- Friedrich Dürrenmatt, *Die Physiker*; *Der Besuch der alten Dame*.
- Max Frisch, *Andorra*.
- Günther Grass, *Die Blechtrommel*; *Katz und Maus*.
- Franz Kafka, *Die Verwandlung*; *Sämtliche Erzählungen*.
- Thomas Mann, *Tonio Kröger*; *Der Tod in Venedig*.
- Bernhard Schlink, *Der Vorleser*.
- Patrick Süskind, *Das Parfum*; *Die Taube*.

German: art

Taschen books are readily available and cheap. Read in English or German. Books are available on the following subjects:

- Bauhaus
- Expressionism
- Wiener Werkstätte.

German: films

Films about the Second World War:

- *Das Boot*
- *Europa, Europa*
- *Die Fälscher*
- *Heimat*

- *Sophie Scholl*
- *Der Untergang.*

Films about the former East Germany:

- *Goodbye Lenin!*
- *Der Himmel über Berlin*
- *Das Leben der Anderen*
- *Sonnenallee*
- *Der Tunnel.*

Italian: reading

- Italo Calvino, *Se una notte d'inverno un viaggiatore.*
- Natalia Ginzburg, *Lessico famigliare.*
- Giuseppe Tomasi di Lampedusa, *Il gattopardo.*
- Primo Levi, *Se questo è un uomo.*
- Luigi Pirandello, *Sei personaggi in cerca d'autore.*
- Leonardo Sciascia, *A ciascuno il suo.*
- Italo Svevo, *La coscienza di Zeno.*

Italian: Films

- *Il Gattopardo*
- *Ladri di Bicilette*
- *Roma, citta aperta*
- *Il vangelo secondo Matteo*

Russian: reading

- Anna Akhmatova, *Requiem.*
- Iosif Brodsky, *Collected Poems in English 1972–1999.*
- Mikhail Bulgakov, *The Master and Margarita.*
- Ivan Bunin, *Life of Arseniev.*
- Anton Chekhov, *Uncle Vanya.*
- Fyodor Dostoevsky, *The Brothers Karamazov; Notes from the Underground.*
- Nikolai Gogol, *Taras Bulba; Diary of a Madman.*
- Mikhail Lermontov, *A Hero of our Time.*
- Boris Pasternak, *Doctor Zhivago.*
- Alexander Pushkin, *Eugene Onegin.*
- Aleksandr Solzhenitsyn, *One Day in the Life of Ivan Denisovich.*
- Leo Tolstoy, *Anna Karenina.*
- Ivan Turgenev, *A Month in the Country.*

Spanish: reading

- *Lazarillo de Tormes.*
- Leopoldo Alas, *La Regenta.*
- Pedro Calderón de la Barca, *La Vida es Sueño.*
- Pio Baroja, *El árbol de la Ciencia.*

- Camilo José Cela, *La Familia de Pascual Duarte*; *La Colmena*.
- Miguel de Cervantes, *El Quijote*.
- Julio Cortázar, *Rayuela*.
- Miguel Delibes, *Cinco Horas con Mario*.
- Rafael Sánchez Ferlosio, *El Jarama*.
- Carmen Martín Gaite, *Lo Raro es Vivir.*
- Juan Goytisolo, *Señas de Identidad*.
- Mario Vargas Llosa, *La Tía Julia y el escribidor.*
- Federico García Lorca, *Poeta en Nueva York*; *La Casa de Bernarda Alba*.
- Carlos Marcial, *El Surrealismo y Cuatro Poetas de la Generación del 27: Ensayo Sobre Extensión y Límites del Surrealismo en la Generación del 27.*
- Javier Marías, *Corazón Tan Blanco*.
- Gabriel García Márquez, *Cien Años de Soledad*.
- Luis Martin-Santos, *Tiempo de Silencio*.
- Ana María Matute, *Olvidado Rey Gudú*.
- Eduardo Mendoza, *La Ciudad de los Prodigios*.
- Pablo Neruda, *Confieso Que he Vivido*.
- Fernando de Rojas, *La Celestina*.
- Miguel de Unamuno, *La Tía Tula*.

Spanish: films

- Pedro Almodóvar, *Todo Sobre mi Madre*
- Jaime Chávarri, *Las Bicicletas son Para el Verano*
- Víctor Erice, *El Espíritu de la Colmena*
- Alejandro González Iñárritu, *Amores Perros*
- Carlos Saura, *Cría Cuervos*; *La Caza*; *Elisa, Vida Mía*.

Music

In addition to reading you should become familiar with the Dover scores of string quartets and symphonies by Haydn, Mozart and Beethoven. Aim to get to know several quartets and symphonies by all three composers.

- Aldwell, E. and Schachter, C., *Harmony and Voice Leading* (3rd edition), Wadsworth Publishing Co., 2002.
- Bohlman, P., *World Music: A Very Short Introduction*, OUP, 2002.
- Caplin, W.E., *Classical Form: A Theory of Formal Functions for the Instrumental Music of Haydn, Mozart, and Beethoven*, OUP, 1998. (This will be invaluable, not only for your analysis studies but also for your understanding of classical-period harmony.)
- Clayton, M., Herbert, T. and Middleton, R., eds, *The Cultural Study of Music: A Critical Introduction*, Routledge, 2003.
- Cook, N., *A Guide to Musical Analysis*, OUP, 1994.

- Cook, N., *Music: A Very Short Introduction*, OUP, 2000.
- Ledbetter, D., ed., *Continuo Playing According to Handel*, Clarendon Press, 1990.
- Morris, R.O. and Ferguson, H., *Preparatory Exercises in Score Reading*, OUP, 1931.
- Parker, R., ed., *The Oxford Illustrated History of Opera*, OUP, 1994.
- Ross, A., *The Rest is Noise*, Fourth Estate, 2008.
- *The New Harvard Dictionary of Music*, Harvard University Press, 1986; or *The Grove Concise Dictionary of Music*, Macmillan, 1988. (Both are useful reference books.)

Harmony and counterpoint

Play and study the following:

- *The Chorale Harmonisations of J.S. Bach*. Recommended edition: Breitkopf and Härtel, ed. B.F. Richter; less good but adequate: Chappell, ed. Albert Riemenschneider.
- 'Fugal Expositions' by J.S. Bach in *The Well-Tempered Clavier* (the '48'). Recommended edition: Associated Board, ed. Richard Jones.
- *Schubert Lieder*. Recommended edition: Dover (either *Schubert's Songs to Texts by Goethe* or *Complete Song Cycles*). The lieder of Beethoven, Mendelssohn, and Schumann are also recommended for your attention.
- *Renaissance polyphony*. Listen to some of the many fine recordings of the music of Palestrina and his contemporaries (the Gimell and Hyperion labels are a rich source).

Natural science (Cambridge)

Biology of cells

- Alberts, B. et al., *Molecular Biology of the Cell*, Taylor & Francis, 2008.

Computer science

- Dewdney, A.K., *The New Turing Omnibus*, Computer Sciences Press, 1993 (reprinted 2001, Henry Holt).
- Körner, Tom W., *The Pleasures of Counting*, CUP, 1996.

Evolution and behaviour

- Barton, N. et al., *Evolution*, Cold Spring Harbour Laboratory Press, 2007.
- Dawkins, R., *The Ancestor's Tale: A Pilgrimage to the Dawn of Life*, Weidenfeld & Nicolson, 2004.

Chemistry

- Atkins, P. and de Paula, J., *Atkins' Physical Chemistry*, OUP, 2009.

- Boyd, Robert N. and Morrison, Robert T., *Organic Chemistry*, Prentice Hall, 1992.
- Cotton, F. Albert et al., *Advanced Inorganic Chemistry*, Wiley, 1999.

Geology (earth sciences)

- Benton, M.J., *When Life Nearly Died*, Thames & Hudson, 2005.
- Ince, M., *Rough Guide to the Earth*, Rough Guides/Penguin, 2007.

Materials science

- Ball, P., *Made to Measure: New Materials for the 21st Century*, Princeton University Press, 1999.
- Cotterill, R.M.J., *The Material World*, CUP, 2008.
- Gordon, J.E., *New Science of Strong Materials*, Penguin, 1991.

Physiology of organisms

- King, J., *Reaching for the Sun*, CUP, 1997.
- Widmaier, E.P., *Why Geese Don't Get Obese (And We Do)*, W.H. Freeman, 2000.

Mathematics

- Gower, T., *Mathematics: A Very Short Introduction*, OUP, 2002.
- Körner, Tom W., *The Pleasures of Counting*, CUP, 1996.
- Petzold, C., *The Annotated Turing*, Wiley Publishing, 2008.
- Russell, B., *Introduction to Mathematical Philosophy*, George Allen and Unwin, 1919.
- Sivia, D.S. and Rawlings, S.G., *Foundations of Science Mathematics*, OUP, 1999.

Elementary mathematics

- Foster, P.C., *Easy Mathematics for Biologists*, CRC, 1999.
- Huff, D., *How to Lie with Statistics*, Penguin, 1991.
- Rowntree, D., *Statistics Without Tears – an Introduction for Non-mathematicians*, Penguin, 2000.

Philosophy

- Alexander, H.G., *The Leibniz–Clarke Correspondence*, Manchester University Press, 1977.
- Ayer, A.J., *The Central Questions of Philosophy*, Penguin, 1976.
- Blackburn, S., *The Big Questions*, Quercus, 2009.
- Bryson, N., *Vision and Painting*, Yale University Press, 1986.
- Dancy, J., *An Introduction to Contemporary Epistemology*, Wiley-Blackwell, 1985.
- Descartes, R., *Discourse on the Method* (many translations).

- Floridi, L., *The 4th Revolution: How the Infosphere is Reshaping Human Reality*, OUP, 2014.
- Hampson, D., *Kierkegaard: Exposition and Critique*, OUP, 2013.
- Hodges, W., *Logic* (2nd revised edition), Penguin, 2001.
- Honderich, T., *The Oxford Companion to Philosophy*, OUP, 1995.
- Hospers, J., *An Introduction to Philosophical Analysis* (4th edition), Routledge, 1997.
- Levinson. J., *The Oxford Handbook of Aesthetics*, OUP, 2005.
- Nagel, T., *What Does it All Mean?*, OUP, 2004.
- O'Hear, A., *What Philosophy Is: An Introduction to Contemporary Philosophy*, Penguin, 1985.
- Runciman, W.G., *Great Books, Bad Arguments*, Princeton University Press, 2010.
- Russell, B., *History of Western Philosophy*, Routledge Classics, 2004.
- Shand, J., *Philosophy and Philosophers*, Acumen, 2002.
- Warburton, N., *Philosophy: The Classics*, Routledge, 2006.
- Williams, B., *Essays and Reviews 1959–2003*, Princeton University Press, 2014.

Physics

- Cullerne, J.P. and Machacek, A., *The Language of Physics*, OUP, 2008.
- Feynman, R.P., *Six Easy Pieces*, Penguin, 1998.
- Feynman, R.P., *Six Not So Easy Pieces*, Penguin, 1999.
- Gribbins, J., *In Search of Schrödinger's Cat – Quantum Physics and Reality*, Black Swan Books, 1991.
- Hawking, S., *A Brief History of Time*, Bantam Press, 1988.

For those with an interest in engineering

- Gordon, J.E., *Structures, or Why Things Don't Fall Down*, DaCapo Press, 2003.
- Gordon, J.E., *The New Science of Strong Materials*, Penguin, 1991.
- Petroski, H., *Invention by Design*, Harvard University Press, 1998.

Politics

- Curtis, M., *The Ambiguities of Power: British Foreign Policy Since 1945*, Zed, 1995.
- Elliott, F. and Hanning, J., *Cameron*, HarperCollins, 2012.
- Hasan, M. and Macintyre, J., eds, *The Milibands and the Making of a Labour Leader*, Biteback, 2011.
- Heffernan, R. et al., eds, *Developments in British Politics 9*, Palgrave Macmillan, 2011.
- McCormick, J., *European Union Politics*, Palgrave Macmillan, 2011.

- McCormick, J., *Contemporary Britain*, Palgrave Macmillan, 2012.
- Vieira, M.B. and Runciman, D., *Representation*, Polity Press, 2008.
- Woolf, J., *An Introduction to Political Philosophy*, OUP, 2006.

Psychology

- Carter, R., *Mapping the Mind*, University of California Press, 2010.
- Coolican, H., *Introduction to Research Methods and Statistics in Psychology*, Psychology Press, 1997.
- Freud, S., *The Psychopathology of Everyday Life* (various editions).
- Goleman, D., *Emotional Intelligence*, Bloomsbury, 1996.
- Gross, R.D., *Psychology: The Science of Mind and Behaviour*, Hodder, 2010.
- Hayes, N., *Foundations of Psychology: Introductory Text* (3rd edition), Cengage Learning EMEA, 2000.
- Hewstone, M., Fincham, F. and Foster, J., *Psychology: British Psychology*, Wiley, 2005.
- Hogg, M., and Vaughan, G., *Social Psychology: An Introduction*, Prentice Hall, 2010.
- Pease, A., *Body Language*, Sheldon Press, 1997.
- Winston, R., *The Human Mind*, Chartered Institute of Personnel and Development, 2006.

TIP!

The Psychologist, a monthly publication of the British Psychological Society, has back issues freely available on its archive at www.thepsychologist.org.uk.

Sociology

- Alexander, J.C. and Thompson, K., *A Contemporary Introduction to Sociology: Culture and Society in Transition*, Paradigm Publishers, 2008.
- Crompton, R., *Class and Stratification* (3rd edition), Polity Press, 2008.
- Giddens, A., *Sociology* (6th edition), Polity Press, 2009.
- Sennett, R., *The Culture of the New Capitalism*, Yale University Press, 2006.

Statistics

- Graham, A., *Teach Yourself Statistics*, McGraw-Hill, 2008.
- Huff, D., *How to Lie with Statistics*, Penguin, 1991.
- Rowntree, D., *Statistics Without Tears – an Introduction for Non-mathematicians*, Penguin, 2000.

Theology

General

- Armstrong, K., *The Case for God*, Vintage, 2010.
- Dawkins, R., *The Blind Watchmaker*, Penguin, 2006.
- Dawkins, R., *The God Delusion*, Black Swan, 2007.
- McGrath, A., *The Dawkins Delusion*, SPCK Publishing, 2007.
- Shortt, R., *Rowan's Rule: The Biography of the Archbishop*, Hodder, 2014.

Biblical

- Bellis, A. Ogden, *Helpmates, Harlots and Heroes*, Westminster/ John Knox Press, 2007.
- Clines, D., *The Theme of the Pentateuch*, Sheffield Academic Press, 1997.
- Lambek, M., ed., *A Reader in the Anthropology of Religion*, Wiley-Blackwell, 2008.
- Painter, J., *The Quest for the Messiah*, Abingdon Press, 1994.
- Vermes, G., *The Changing Faces of Jesus*, Penguin, 2001.

History and doctrine

- St Augustine, *City of God*.
- St Augustine, *The Confessions.*
- Duffy, E., *The Stripping of the Altars*, Yale University Press, 2005.
- Gunton, C.E., *The One, the Three and the Many*, CUP, 1993.
- McCulloch, D., *Silence: A Christian History*, Allen Lane, 2013.
- McGrath, A., *Reformation Thought* (4th edition), Wiley-Blackwell, 2012.
- McGrath, A., *Modern Christian Thought*, Wiley-Blackwell, 1995.

Further resources

In addition to the suggestions above, remember to:

- read around your subject in the press
- search for podcasts and videos
- check out blogs and online articles
- if possible, discuss your reading with friends, family and teachers.

5 | Choosing your university and college

So you've decided that you want to apply. You're studying the right A levels, you are predicted or already have the appropriate grades and you've been reading around your subject. What next?

As an undergraduate, you may only apply to either Oxford **or** Cambridge, and therefore, you need to decide which. You should try to make an educated choice; ideally do your research and visit both, have a look round the various colleges and university buildings and drink in the atmosphere. Talk to friends who are currently at Oxbridge and teachers who have been there. You also need to understand the courses each university offers; for example, Cambridge offers natural sciences in place of physics, chemistry or biology; politics, philosophy and economics (PPE) is unique to Oxford, as is human, social and political sciences (HSPS) to Cambridge.

Which university?

There are several reasons to choose one university over the other but the most important aspect to consider is whether it offers you the right course. Oxford and Cambridge agree that the most important decision a prospective applicant has to make is the degree they wish to study, not which university they want to apply to. Both universities are committed to recruiting the most talented students regardless of their background and both are world class in teaching and research in both arts and science subjects.

First, choose your course

It is essential to check that the university you prefer teaches the subject you wish to study. There are various subjects that Oxford offers which Cambridge does not and vice versa.

Subjects you can study at **Cambridge** but not at Oxford include:

- architecture
- Asian and Middle Eastern studies

- economics (as a stand-alone subject; at Oxford economics is offered only as a combined course with management, engineering and management, materials and management, history or as an element of the PPE degree course)
- education
- human, social and political science (HSPS)
- land economy
- Anglo-Saxon, Norse and Celtic
- management studies (as a stand-alone subject; at Oxford you do management as a combined course with economics, engineering and economics or materials and economics)
- natural sciences (at Oxford all the sciences are offered but not in the same combination)
- philosophy (as a stand-alone subject; at Oxford you do philosophy as a combined course such as PPE or physics and philosophy)
- veterinary medicine.

Subjects you can study at **Oxford** but not at Cambridge include:

- archaeology and anthropology (as a stand-alone subject; at Cambridge you can choose to do the subjects as part of the HSPS course)
- human sciences (as a stand-alone subject; at Cambridge human sciences is incorporated into the HSPS course)
- the languages Sanskrit and Czech with Slovak
- Oriental studies
- PPE
- psychology, philosophy and linguistics
- separate sciences (although you may have to take modules in other science subjects as well).

Subjects you can study at **both** universities include:

- classics
- computer science
- engineering
- English literature and language
- geography
- history
- law
- modern and medieval languages
- music
- psychology
- theology and religious studies.

It is important to note that, although many subjects are the same, their components may differ between the two universities and you should take time to compare the courses in detail.

For more information go to the websites listed below:

- Cambridge: www.study.cam.ac.uk/undergraduate/courses
- Oxford: www.ox.ac.uk/admissions/undergraduate_courses/ courses/index.html.

Course flexibility

At Oxford, most subjects include compulsory courses for the first year, and then give students the opportunity to choose options in subsequent years. At Cambridge, courses cover the subject very broadly in the initial years and then become more specialised within a wide range of options in the later years.

Comparing the Tripos system at Cambridge with the two-part system at Oxford can be another way to help you decide which university is better suited to you. One of the great attractions of Cambridge is the flexibility of its Tripos system (the name Tripos is said to have been derived from the three-legged stool that undergraduates in the Middle Ages sat on at graduation ceremonies).

Each course, or Tripos, is usually divided into two parts: Part I and Part II. After each part there is an exam that counts towards your final under-graduate mark. A Part I can take one year (in economics, for example) or two years (in English). A two-year Part I is divided into Part IA and Part IB. Once you have completed Part I (A and B), you have the option of continuing to specialise in the same subject, or swapping to a related but different subject for Part II.

In theory, this gives students quite a bit of flexibility, and there have been students who have studied three different but related subjects during the course of their three years at Cambridge and have come out with a First Class degree. In reality, however, you should not go to your inter-view thinking that you will be able to change courses easily. Admissions tutors, particularly those interviewing for humanities, arts and social sci-ences, will see this as a sign that a student is not committed to their subject, and give the place to someone who is. If students want to change subject when they get to Cambridge they have to work very hard at convincing their current director of studies (DOS) that they want to change for the right reasons. Then students have to convince the DOS in their new subject to take them on.

On the other hand, there are subjects where elongated undergraduate degrees are encouraged. Natural sciences and mathematics students have the option of adding a Part III, while engineering students take Parts IA, IB, IIA and IIB over four years, leading ultimately to the award of MEng.

The system works slightly differently at Oxford. As at Cambridge, students have to pass exams in two parts. However, students do not have to take examinations at the end of each year, as is the case in many Cambridge courses. The Preliminary Examinations (or 'Prelims') are taken at the end of the first year (apart from a few exceptions) and the Final Examinations ('Finals') are taken at the end of the third year. Most arts and social science undergraduates at Oxford University do not take exams in their second year; maths and science students take exams at the end of each year.

In general there are more courses at Oxford that are designed to take four years. The Joint Honours courses of mathematics and philosophy and physics and philosophy, as well as classics, take four years. Mathematics itself, physics and earth sciences can take either three or four years (your choice), but in the case of molecular and cellular biochemistry, chemistry, engineering and metallurgy, students are normally expected to progress to the fourth, research-based year leading to the award of a master's degree.

You should research the similarities and differences that apply to your particular subject choice carefully, and then be prepared to discuss your discoveries when it comes to the interview stage.

Case study: Silvester, Queen's College, Cambridge

What I really appreciate about studying at Cambridge is the opportunities I have been given to develop my passion for my subject, archaeology and anthropology. For example, this year I was fortunate enough to be able to participate in an excavation in Tajikistan. What follows is a report of my time on the dig, which also gives an idea of the type of work a Cambridge student may be expected to produce.

The archaeological site, Panjakent, is a 5th–8th century AD mud brick city situated in the Sugd Province of north-western Tajikistan. The geography of the area is defined by snow-capped mountains (exceeding 5,000 metres in elevation), cut through by the high-velocity Zarafshan River. At Panjakent, the Zarafshan eventually incorporates a floodplain prior to its disappearance/ evaporation in the deserts of Uzbekistan. The local climate is of a 'dry continental' nature, with warm summers, cold winters and limited precipitation. As a result, irrigation was and still is key to human settlements in the region, allowing for the cultivation of grain, the tending of orchards and grazing animals.

Until the expansion of Islam, the Zarafshan valley, together with the neighbouring Samarkand and Bukhara regions of Uzbekistan, was run by various semi-autonomous Sogdian polities. These can trace their origins back to the 5th century Achaemenid expansion. As a result, the ancient inhabitants of Panjakent are associated with Iranian people, their Sogdian language being classified as a Persian dialect.

The city itself was in use at a time when trade along the 'Silk Road' was at its height. With regard to this, Russian archaeologists who worked in the region often interpret a situation in which Sogdian polities acted as 'middle-men', exchanging Mediterranean/Middle Eastern goods, for Uighur (the indigenous people of what is now the Xiangjiang province of China) as well as Chinese trade items, from the Far East (Vaissière 2005). This is not only supported by Panjakent's strategic position along the east–west Zarafshan axis, but also by numerous Chinese and Arabic Texts – the writings of the Chinese Buddhist Pilgrim Monk Xuanjaung being such an example (Vaissière 2005). Furthermore, the uncovering of Sogdian texts, listing economic transactions (the exchange of Sasanian silver ware, alfalfa, Baltic amber for Chinese silk) found in places as far away as Kashgar, truly supports this merchant image, and suggests that the Sogdian dialect was the 'lingua franca' of the Silk Road.

This 'golden' Sogdian era lasted until the early 8th century, when the Arabic conqueror Said al-Harashi laid siege to various Sogdian towns as part of the spread of Islam. Thus, in the year AD722 Panjakent was besieged and burnt. The following centuries saw Persian/Sogdian culture becoming increasingly 'mixed' with Arabic, Muslim traditions.

The destruction (through fire) and relatively quick abandonment of the city has facilitated its superb preservation, uncompromised by human intervention. The easily erodible clay (transported by wind and colluvium) from nearby mountainsides was able to quickly cover the settlement area in the state in which it was left. This has helped keep streets, arches, towers, wall reliefs, carbonised organic material, and houses up to two storeys high sheltered from the elements. Thus when the site was rediscovered by Soviet archaeologists, Panjakent was nicknamed the 'Pompeii of Central Asia'.

The Panjakent excavations have been undertaken by the St Petersburg Hermitage museum every year since 1947. Due to this, almost 50% of Panjakant has already been uncovered, thereby allowing for the estimation that Panjakent was originally 20 hectares in size, with a population of 5,000 people. A lot of the finds and data obtained so far reflect the city's unique location and role in central Asia. For instance, the walled town and fortified citadel of Panjakent, together with further outposts extending eastwards along the Zarafshan Range, demonstrate how the Sogdians were in strong control of the trade caravan routes and high mountain passes. In addition, the uncovering of Buddhist texts, and wall paintings depicting Shaivist deities, show how Panjakent was incorporated in the cultural spread of ideas throughout Asia (e.g. Sogdians also operated as translators, for example, translating the Buddhist Sutra texts from the Indian subcontinent into Chinese (Vaissière 2005). Nevertheless, this year's substantial uncovering of funeral pyres once again suggests that Zoroastrianism was the main religion, thereby affirming the close Persian cultural link.

A major feature during the excavation was distinguishing deposited clay from clay/mud bricks, which formed the built structures of the town. As a result, techniques were significantly different from those used in British archaeology. For instance, this year the volunteers would frequently work with hammers and adzes in order to gradually 'knock' away naturally deposited layers from mud-brick structures. At the beginning it is often difficult to distinguish between the two; however with practice one was able to gradually feel, and hear, the difference.

The Russian team stressed the importance of uncovering pottery, and every afternoon we occupied ourselves with the restoration of ceramic artefacts. This desire to complete the excavation with as many intact pieces as possible may once again have reflected the team's interest in typology, in order to identify different artefacts arguably coming from different cultural groups. This would highlight the importance of trade. However it also shows how cultural-historical interpretations have a much stronger voice outside of Anglophone archaeology.

In the former Soviet Union, Panjakent's claim to fame was its elaborate wall paintings and frescoes. These were once again of great importance during this year's excavation, since a substantial number were uncovered. A lot of time was thus spent painstakingly cleaning, drawing, removing these images from uncovered walls and artificially preserving them through various chemical treatments. Since however Tajikistan is now independent, this raised serious questions about Russian and Tajik heritage. One was frequently confronted with the fact that Russian archaeologists were the first to discover Panjakent, at a time when Tajikistan was part of the Soviet Union – thereby explaining why the majority of frescoes are now exhibited in the St Petersburg Hermitage museum. At the same time, whilst frescoes uncovered today are required to remain in Tajikistan, both local and Russian academics still doubt as to whether or not the Dushanbe Museum is capable of ensuring adequate protection and preservation. This strengthens the case that such artefacts should be once again taken care of by Russia. From one point of view this would see the Heritage value shift, from something as symbolic of Tajik/Persian/Sogdian identity, to a symbol of the project achievements of the Hermitage museum.

In terms of built structures, this year involved digging test pits near the Eastern Gate of the town. This eventually led to the uncovering of what was interpreted as two granaries and a house. During this process, geochemical surveying played a significant role, contributing to the identification of earlier destruction/burnt layers prior to AD722. Occurring on a small scale at the east side of Panjakent, these layers make clear 'earlier continuation' harder to identify, thereby raising the possibility that the built structures we uncovered could have originally had a different use.

In conclusion, Panjakent as an archaeological site stands out due to its strategic location in central Asia, connecting the Far East to the Middle East and Mediterranean worlds. It is also unique in that its destruction, abandonment and quick burial under clay deposits allowed for great preservation. This allowed our team to once again access a great amount of data.

Bibliography

de la Vaissière, E., *Sogdian Traders: A History*, Leiden, Brill, 2005

Other factors to consider

The location

Oxford is located about 100km (62 miles) north-west of London, with excellent links to the capital and the rest of the country by car, coach and train. It is a lively, medium-sized city with a total student population of over 30,000 (including students at both Oxford and Oxford Brookes). Most university and college buildings are located in the centre and are easily reached on foot or by bike.

Cambridge lies 88.5km (55 miles) north of London, off the M11 motorway, and is a 45-minute journey by train from the capital. There are also excellent rail links to Scotland and the north of England (via Peterborough), with direct regional services from Birmingham, the Midlands, East Anglia and the north-west of England. The city is also very well served by bus services to and from other cities. Stansted Airport is 48km (30 miles) away. The city has also become the centre of the hi-tech 'silicon Fen' industries. It is much smaller than Oxford and this can make Cambridge feel claustrophobic for some, but there are plenty of open green spaces in this undeniably beautiful place.

The student mix

Oxford has an undergraduate ratio of 54% male and 46% female. The percentages for all students are 62% home and 38% overseas (undergraduates: 84% home; 16% overseas). The University's intake from state schools is 56.8% of undergraduates.

Cambridge's profile is very similar: 53% male, 47% female; a state school intake (undergraduates) of 63.3%; and 24% of students are international students.

Teaching

Teaching methods are very similar at both universities, as students will attend lectures, classes and laboratory work, as appropriate for their course. Unlike at many other universities, students at Oxford and Cambridge also benefit from one-to-one teaching from world experts in their field. The only difference is in the name: Oxford refers to these sessions as 'tutorials' while Cambridge calls them 'supervisions'.

Assessment

Students at Oxford and Cambridge are assessed informally throughout their course by producing work for their tutors/supervisors for weekly tutorials/supervisions. Formal assessment is almost entirely based on examinations, although in the final year of many courses one examination paper can be replaced with a dissertation.

At Oxford, the final degree classification result is usually based on the examinations taken at the end of the final year. Cambridge students, in contrast, are assessed through examinations in more than one year of their courses.

Research standards

Oxford has more world-leading academics than any other UK university (rated 4* in the 2008 national Research Assessment Exercise). It has consistently boasted the highest research income from external sponsors of any UK university (in 2012–13 40% (£436.8m) of income came from this source), and receives the highest level of quality research funding from the Higher Education Funding Council for England (HEFCE).

Cambridge is equally blessed financially, and performance league tables consistently place Cambridge among the world's top-ranking institutions.

International reputation

In the 2014 Academic Ranking of World Universities published by the Shanghai Jiao Tong University, Cambridge was placed fifth globally for academic and research performance and Oxford was positioned in ninth place, placing both institutions at the forefront of the most prestigious universities in the world.

Availability of part-time work

Oxford offers opportunities for a limited amount of paid work within college, for which you may need your tutor's permission, and colleges sometimes offer employment during the summer conference season. The University Careers Service facilitates summer internship and work opportunities through the Oxford University International Internship Programme and on-campus employer events and fairs.

Cambridge states that since the university terms are short and highly demanding on students' time and intellectual capabilities, it strongly discourages taking on part-time work. However, as a Cambridge undergraduate, you will find it relatively easy to procure internships and holiday work if you are prepared to put enough effort into researching and applying.

Which college?

Your next decision is which college to choose. Many students are thrown into a complete quandary about this and at first sight it seems hard to know how to decide. Your college will be the centre of your academic and social life and it is worth putting a bit of thought into why you might prefer one over another.

Oxford and Cambridge colleges are independent, self-governing communities of academics, students and staff. The collegiate system gives students and academics the benefits of belonging to both a large, internationally renowned institution and a smaller, interdisciplinary, academic college community. Colleges and halls enable leading academics and students across subjects and year groups and from different cultures and countries to work and socialise together. This system gives you the opportunity to discuss your work in college tutorials and seminars, over meals in the dining hall or in your college accommodation late into the evening, and it will provide you with the chance to establish a new circle of friends quickly, and to access a range of varied social and sporting activities.

Your college will have a senior tutor whose role includes general oversight of all undergraduate members of the college, although your academic studies will be directed by your department or faculty. The relatively small number of students at each college allows for close and supportive personal attention to be given to the induction, academic development and welfare of individual students. Each student has a college adviser, who is a member of the college's academic staff and will be able to offer support and advice.

Open application

If you cannot decide which college to apply to, it is possible to make an open application. An open application is where you do not choose a college; instead, you are assigned to one by the admissions board. Allocation is often to 'less popular' colleges; this does not make them bad colleges, simply colleges that have fewer applicants than others in the current cycle of applications. Both universities stress that making an open application in no way disadvantages you.

You may decide to make an open application if you really don't mind what your college life will be like. However, college life is such a great and unique aspect of Oxbridge that it's well worth at least putting some thought into it. As making an open application does not disadvantage you, don't be afraid to take this route if you really feel it is best for you.

If you decide not to make an open application, the next step is to narrow down the list of 31 colleges at Cambridge and 38 colleges (and six permanent private halls) at Oxford to make your personal shortlist from which you will make your final choice.

How do I choose a college that is right for me?

You might consider any or all of the following factors when making your decision.

Does it offer the right course?

Some colleges will have a great reputation for certain courses (such as Balliol for PPE, for instance) and some will not offer every course offered by the universities.

To find out which colleges offer your course, you can see a comprehensive list at www.oxbridgecolleges.com.

Do you want to be with a certain type of student?

A minority of colleges admit only certain groups of students, so if you want to be in a women-only college or with more mature or graduate students your options are limited.

Women only: Murray Edwards (formerly New Hall), Newnham and Lucy Cavendish at Cambridge.

Mature students (over 21 at matriculation) only: Hughes Hall, Lucy Cavendish, St Edmund's and Wolfson at Cambridge; Harris Manchester at Oxford.

Graduates only: Clare Hall and Darwin at Cambridge; Green Templeton, Kellogg, Linacre, Nuffield, St Antony's, St Cross and Wolfson at Oxford.

Does it have the right character?

There's no question that each college has its distinct character, whether it is highly academic, sporty or literary. Certainly, there is an element of 'horses for courses', if you'll pardon the pun. Being with like-minded students may make you work harder, but if you're the kind of person who would rather come out with a 2.i and have captained a sports team or run student societies than strive for a First, then you may want to pick somewhere that will be sympathetic to your aspirations.

Every year, Oxford publishes the Norrington table and Cambridge the Tompkins table (see Appendix 3), which rank the colleges in order of the number of First Class degrees achieved by their students in their final exams. This may give you some indication of the colleges' academic prowess. But beware of placing too much importance on this; colleges go up and down the tables at an alarming rate and those at the top of the tables one year may find themselves halfway down the next.

What are the admissions criteria?

The colleges all have different admissions criteria for the subjects they offer. In addition to the information provided by your UCAS application, some colleges will request some sample work and some will require candidates to sit a test at interview. You need to read the admissions criteria for your course very carefully and this may help you decide. You might find that there are admissions criteria you aren't comfortable with or even highlight colleges whose criteria particularly appeal to you.

Is the location convenient?

It's definitely worth locating your faculty buildings and lecture halls and seeing which colleges are nearby. This may sound faintly ridiculous when most of the colleges are located quite centrally, but you will be delighted to be able to fall out of bed and be at your lecture within 10 minutes of waking up after a hard night of working or playing. Bear in mind that a lot of people cycle around Oxford and Cambridge, so you may wish to consider cycling distance and walking distance.

Equally important is the college's location generally: consider what facilities are nearby, and whether you'd rather be right in the middle of it all or somewhere with more space to yourself.

Does it have the right facilities?

At this stage it might be useful to consult the alternative prospectus provided by students at each university (these can be found on every college website). Students already at Oxbridge are expert at discussing their own college's good and bad points. Once you have read them, you can eliminate colleges that don't have a particular facility (such as provision for sports or music). If you're unsure, contact the college directly for clarification. You may think now that all you will do at university is work, but you will be grateful that your college has extra facilities such as a decent JCR bar with ping-pong tables or playing fields nearby or a fantastic music venue. You may not necessarily want to row for the university but you might have fun rowing for your college, for example. It's worth doing a bit of research into what colleges offer before you make a decision.

Should I visit the college and check it out?

If you can, you should. Just a wander round the grounds and a look at the current students will probably give you a feeling that a college is or isn't right for you, and you are bound to prefer some over others. If you are unable to attend an open day, it is still possible to get a feel for a college by visiting at another time, although you may be restricted in terms of which areas you can explore. You can also ask questions of current students and professors. Each college has its own printed prospectus, which will provide more detailed information than its entry in the university prospectus.

Should I think about the accommodation?

You'll be spending three or four years at university and the standard of college accommodation varies quite dramatically from college to college. If the size and standard of room matters to you, a bit of research will pay dividends. What's more, some colleges offer accommodation for the whole of your course, whereas at others you may find yourself competing against everyone else in the private rental sector (and 'living out' can prove more costly as you will have to rent a flat or house for the whole of the academic year, not just during term time).

Should I make a tactical decision?

So you're nearly there. You're close to deciding on your choice of university and your course. Lots of people now try to make a tactical choice based on which colleges are less popular, less centrally located, less well endowed; the theory being that somehow they'll be easier to get into. But don't be fooled. There is no clever way around the system. Don't waste any time worrying about it.

Just because a college is smaller or out of the way (such as Girton at Cambridge) or has fewer applicants per place offered (such as St Hilda's at Oxford), you should not think that this will give you a higher chance of a place. Although a few colleges often receive less than one applicant per place offered (check the Oxford admissions website, for example), it does not mean that every direct applicant is offered a place, merely that many of their successful applicants come from the pooling system. Both Oxford and Cambridge put a lot of effort into inter-college 'moderation' to ensure that your chances do not depend on which college you applied to. You might be the only applicant to your chosen college for your chosen course and still not be offered a place. Choose your first preference based on where you think you might be happy, rather than on where you think you have the 'best' chance.

Case study: Lucy, Balliol College, Oxford

Your relationship with your tutors is one of the most important aspects of the Oxford education system; you become very close on a personal and academic level. Because most if not all of your tutorials take place in your college, you become even more closely linked to your college. In my case, this is Balliol and I have found the set-up to be very beneficial. This is actually a really good thing: they will always be looking out for your welfare and have a really good understanding of how you think and learn, meaning that you are looked after in a way a lot of other universities don't provide. The fact that they are on site at Balliol means that they are very accessible too.

The same goes for the collegiate system in general. In first year everyone lives in college – the population mix of the other students (i.e. whether second and third years live in college) depends on the college itself, but there is always a mix, which means you meet a lot of different people of a range of years, ages and subjects studied. There is a strong feel of community, and opportunities to meet and interact with each other in hall, the JCR (Junior Common Room, which is both a physical place as well as the political college student body), the bar and college bops (college parties every fortnight). I think this is a hugely beneficial system for meeting lots of different people, and it's a lovely, tight-knit community. It's hard to feel alienated in such a system, it's really like one big family, and there is a huge network of welfare support run by the JCR, including women's officers, ethnic minorities and overseas officers and so on.

Having said that, it is very easy to mix with people from other colleges through drama, sport, going out and so on. Your college does not define who you are, but provides a nice base from which to explore the university as a whole.

In terms of work, it must be said: there is a fair amount! But that is to be expected and if you love what you're doing then it pays off. The teaching system is mostly based on tutorials: one-on-one or two-on-one sessions with a tutor for an hour each week. It is an intense but highly fruitful way of learning, with your tutors really being able to respond to your ideas. The format is one of an informal conversation, there are no 'sirs' or 'misses', and it is relaxed but exhilarating.

Lectures are more important for some subjects than others – for sciences, especially medicine, for example, they are compulsory, and more teaching is done in labs. For the humanities, in contrast, there is more emphasis on seminars.

6 | Experience to support your application

Everything about your Oxbridge application needs to be convincing if you are to present yourself in the best possible light. We have already discussed the importance of being able to show that you have read around your subject and that you have delved far beyond the standard exam texts in your desire to find out more about your subject. But what else can you do that will set your application apart?

Work experience is essential if you think you want to study a vocational subject such as law or medicine, and it is important that you explore how you are going to organise this well in advance. It is naïve to think that you can arrange work experience at short notice; you will need to ask the advice of your parents, friends and school to help you arrange something worthwhile and you must plan ahead. Ideally you will have arranged several bursts of relevant work experience.

It is important to keep your eyes and ears open to relevant events that you could attend in your area, newspaper articles that relate to your subject, blogs, radio programmes and any other sources of information that might give your application an additional dimension. A whole range of companies have in the past offered gap-year programmes; for example, the big four accountancy firms (PricewaterhouseCoopers, KPMG, Deloitte, Accenture), as well as IBM, the Bank of England and Rothschild. There is also The Year in Industry, which specialises in a broad range of year-long gap-year placements.

Gap years

There has been much debate recently about the value of gap years. You will need to decide whether to make an application for deferred entry (this is when you apply while doing your A levels, two years in advance of your first term at university) or to apply a year after your school friends do, while you are on your year out. When making this decision you should ring your college of choice to discuss its preferences.

Can I take a gap year and defer my entry?

Some Cambridge and Oxford colleges do not like making offers to deferred entrants, simply because this means they have to commit a place before they have met competing applicants for the following year. In this case, colleges encourage you to wait a year and apply while on your gap year. If you ask their advice and make the most of your time out, you will find that most colleges are happy for you to have a gap year. In allowing yourself time to mature you may even make a better application and become a more attractive candidate. But you should be aware that if you apply pre-A level and ask for a gap year, you may be swaying your odds of being offered a place against you. It is always best to check with the college to which you are thinking of applying as to its policy before deciding on deferred entry or not.

Cambridge states that about one in 10 students take a gap year before starting their studies. It acknowledges that a year out can be a very useful time in which to improve skills, earn money, travel and generally gain maturity and self-reliance. It asks that you state on your UCAS application if you wish to defer entry. You'll almost certainly be asked about your plans at interview, so you need to be prepared to talk about what you hope to do and achieve in your gap year.

If you're applying for mathematics, most colleges have a preference for immediate entry. However, if you're applying for engineering, many colleges generally prefer applicants to take a year out, to gain some industrial experience. You will not be able to defer entry for the graduate course in medicine.

What about Oxford? Some commentators will say that it isn't true that you can't get in if you take a gap year; for instance, in 2012 Oxford made 6.4% of offers to gap-year students, with 6.7% of applicants applying to start post-gap year. This is an insignificant difference, demonstrating that taking a gap year may do your chances of getting an offer no harm. However, if you do opt to take a gap year, it is important that you choose to do something worthwhile, ideally which emphasises your enthusiasm for the subject.

It's important to understand that each college has a different point of view about gap years and you must check the college's website to ensure that you know what its opinion is. For example, here's what Merton College says:

> 'Applications for deferred entry are welcomed for all subjects
> taken by the College, except Physics and the beginners' Russian
> course. Candidates should be aware that in many subjects,
> applicants who are offered places for deferred entry will generally
> be among the strongest of the cohort for their subject. A number
> of deferred entry applicants may be offered a non-deferred place

instead. For more detail on individual subjects' deferred entry policies, please check departmental websites.'

Some tutors in physics do not encourage deferred entry, largely because lack of practice can affect the mathematical competence achieved at A level or equivalent. They will, however, consider applications in certain special circumstances, e.g. where a candidate sponsored by industry is spending a year in a laboratory.

It is very helpful if all applicants planning a gap year explain briefly what their plans entail on their application form.

Work experience

What kind of work experience is best?

Any kind of work experience will be useful. Just getting used to the routine of working in an office, shop, restaurant or factory can come as quite a shock. Getting to work on time, dressing appropriately, getting on with your work colleagues, coping with boredom as well as stress are all valuable lessons in life skills.

Ideally, though, you should try to find work experience that relates to the subject you hope to study at university. Experience within the work environment is particularly important if you want to study a vocational subject, for example law or medicine. It is often only in a work situation that one can fully understand the stresses, responsibilities and pleasures that go along with a particular career, and only then can you really commit. Work experience can provide admissions tutors with strong evidence that candidates are committed, determined and have thought through their applications carefully. It can also provide you with a goal that keeps you motivated even through the toughest periods of study.

Apart from having a real idea of where you might be in five years' time, work experience can expose you to ideas relating to the subject you are about to study in exciting ways. For example, if you want to study a science subject at Oxford or Cambridge, you might try to get a week during school holidays helping or observing at a laboratory where the scientists are working on something you are particularly interested in. You will be able to sit in on lab meetings and hear for yourself the problems that they face and the solutions they come to. You can also ask them personally for reading suggestions. No one will be as ahead of the game as they are, and this will give you some really exciting things to discuss at interview.

If you are really serious about studying and learning, find a way to get more information within the work environment. This will not only give you greater knowledge and confidence, it will also show the admissions tutors that you are really interested.

How do I organise my work experience?

It's never too early to start planning your work experience and the really ambitious student will aim to organise several sessions.

It will be difficult in the current economic climate to persuade companies to let you join them, but if you are persistent and imaginative you will find openings.

First, do your research. Search online to find out about companies and institutions that operate in your field of study. What about think tanks and other, more academic organisations or publishing houses that produce literature for your chosen subject?

Next, find someone in your chosen organisation to contact. Never send a letter to a company or organisation without finding an appropriate person to address it to; the more senior, the better. Letters that are sent without a specific recipient usually end up in the accounts department!

Write a winning introductory letter. Say exactly what you're looking for in terms of job opportunities, when you want to join and what you feel you can offer the company.

Attach the perfect CV. Brief, accurate, with no typing errors or grammatical or spelling mistakes.

Include a couple of references. Perhaps one from a teacher at your school and one from another responsible adult who has been impressed by your resourcefulness or past endeavours.

Email a few days after you've posted your letters. Quite often, your email will go straight to the relevant person if you type their full name with a stop in the middle and then their company name, e.g. joe.brown@ multinational.com. It is worth a try!

Follow up. If you haven't had a response, phone a week later and ask if they received your application. Be very polite. Good luck!

Case study: Julia, Archaeology and Anthropology, Pembroke College, Oxford

I have always been very interested in archaeology and anthropology, but in the years preceding my university application I had mostly just read about the subject. However, in my AS year, as I was deciding that the subject was one that I definitely wanted to study at university, I thought it would be best for me to get some practical experience to see whether it was definitely for me. I also knew that the practical element was important.

During that summer, I returned to my home country of China. My town is an ancient one with a great deal of history and tradition, so before I returned I wrote to my local cultural museum to see whether they needed any volunteers, especially English-speaking ones who could work with the many tourists from England and other countries where English is spoken. Fortunately, I was a good fit for the museum as they needed English-speaking guides. I was really in my element.

I also entered a competition for a travel fund that my college was running. I wrote about a special project I wanted to do, working in a village in Cambodia, observing the customs of the local ethnic group and reporting back on these. I was awarded a sum of money to pay for some of my costs and in return I had to write up some of my findings for the college magazine.

I found both of these experiences to be very rewarding and they really helped to prepare me for my course at university.

Events in your subject area

If you want to study a humanities subject, particularly a subject that is not vocational, keeping up to date with current affairs and events in your area is perhaps even more important than work experience. If you are really passionate about your subject, and dedicated to getting a place at Oxford or Cambridge, you should be constantly on the look-out for local events that are relevant to the subject that you want to study. Local libraries often host talks by renowned authors, the Royal Institution and the Science Museum in London host regular science lectures, the Royal Geographical Society organises regular discussions with eminent geographers and the Royal Academy of Arts has an ongoing art history lecture series. In addition, the universities in your area may hold lectures that could interest you. Speak to your teachers for ideas or go online to search for relevant events.

Ideas you might consider include:

- politics: go on a tour of the Houses of Parliament
- law: sit in the public gallery of your local magistrates' or Crown court
- history and archaeology: visit the British Museum
- art and history of art: visit every gallery and museum you can get to, including the galleries local to Oxford and Cambridge, such as the Ashmolean in Oxford and the Fitzwilliam in Cambridge.

You should also be aware of news stories that relate to developments in your field. Try to get as big a picture as possible of your subject: about how it relates to the rest of the world and why it might be important to know about it. Keep up to date with relevant blogs and think tanks, read the newspapers online and listen to podcasts.

Case study: Violet, History of Art, Cambridge

I was lucky enough to study at a sixth-form college in central London, which was near many museums and art galleries. For example, the Victoria and Albert Museum was only a few minutes' walk away and I was able to visit it frequently, not only formally on visits arranged by my history of art tutor, but also when I had some free periods. I made a point of jotting down notes in my journal, which I was then able to refer back to when writing my personal statement.

I also frequently visited the National Gallery and the Courtauld. My tutor was able to recommend some very pertinent wider reading, which really focused my mind. History of Art trips to Florence and Paris were also really beneficial in enhancing my knowledge of the subject and really ignited my passion for studying it at university. My other A level subjects, English Literature and Spanish, complemented my studies in History of Art, so I felt very well prepared by the time I was called for interview.

I really enjoyed my course at Cambridge, which enabled me to grow as a person. I was very successful and went on to study for an MA in History of Art. I am now embarking on a career in the field through teaching, which I am really excited about.

7| The UCAS application and the personal statement

So finally you are ready to apply. The next stage is arguably the one that causes students the most anxiety. Your UCAS application will need to be submitted by the closing date for all Oxbridge applications of 6p.m. on 15 October.

Let's go through the practicalities step by step.

Step one: preparing your UCAS application

The online form will be the same as for every other university: through the University and Colleges Admissions Service (UCAS). The UCAS form is a long document that is completed online and sent to all five of your chosen universities. It asks you to include details of your school(s), exam grades, employment experience, your choices of university in order of preference and a personal statement: a 47-line written document that outlines the reasons for your choice of subject.

We will look more closely at what makes a winning personal statement later in this chapter.

You will need to specify a campus code in your 'courses' section. For most universities, this will be 'main site', but for collegiate universities such as Cambridge and Oxford, you need to state the college you wish to apply to from the list, or select 'Open' if you are not concerned about naming a specific college.

Step two: references

You will need to tell your school or college that you wish to apply to Oxbridge as soon as possible. If it has had lots of candidates who have applied before, the staff will be aware of what the colleges are looking for from the academic reference. If your school has little experience of making Oxbridge applications, the universities will probably be aware of this anyway and base their decision more on your personal statement and grades. But it is worth reminding your referees of the early deadline and making sure they'll have your reference ready on time.

You will also need to confirm that your school has submitted the Extenuating Circumstances Form to Cambridge, if you are eligible to apply through this scheme (see pages 15–16).

Step three: external tests

You must check whether the universities require you to sit any special tests such as the BMAT or the National Admissions Test for Law (LNAT). See Chapter 8 for more details.

Step four: supplementary questionnaires

Cambridge

Once you've submitted your UCAS form, you will receive an acknowledgement almost immediately from Cambridge by email, along with its Supplementary Application Questionnaire (SAQ), which will require completion by the following week.

The SAQ is filled out online, costs nothing to send and gives Cambridge more information about you and your application. If you do not have access to email you can contact the Cambridge admissions office for a paper version.

The initial email will give you all the information you need in order to complete the form correctly, as well as a deadline (usually the end of October).

The SAQ includes the following eight sections.

1. **Photograph.** You will need a passport-sized colour photograph of yourself, preferably in digital format, which can then be uploaded onto the form.
2. **Application type.** This section asks questions about your application, such as whether you have applied for an organ scholarship, if you are taking a gap year or whether you are including the Extenuating Circumstances Form.
3. **Personal details.** This covers information about you and your own situation, such as where you live, what your first name is, etc.
4. **Course details.** Here you need to declare your preferred course options (if applicable); for example, if you are applying to read modern and medieval languages, you state which languages you wish to study in this section.

5. **Education.** In this section, you will need to give information about your school(s), such as class sizes and descriptions of any extra help you may have received towards your application.
6. **Qualifications.** In this section, you need to give details of your AS and/or A level modules, or their equivalents, and your marks.
7. **Additional information.** This is where you can add an additional personal statement. You will also need to discuss your career plans and give some proof of your interest in your chosen subject (for example, details of your work experience).
8. **Submit.**

The additional personal statement is the perfect opportunity for you to explain to the admissions tutor how excited you are about the course and perhaps the college to which you are applying. Do take advantage of this extra space to make an impression.

Remember, however, not to duplicate anything you have said on the UCAS form. While your UCAS personal statement will be seen by every institution you apply to, the SAQ is for the admissions tutors at Cambridge only. This means that you can discuss particular elements of the course content or programme at Cambridge without putting any other university off. Make the most of this and explain why its course and teaching staff are perfect for you, and why you will fit in particularly well there.

Remember also that by mentioning your areas of special academic interest, you will encourage predictable questions at interview, making it easier to prepare thoroughly.

Oxford

Your chosen college at Oxford will usually be fairly swift in confirming that it has received your application and it will write requesting any further information it requires. If you have made an open application, the college to which you have been allocated will respond.

Oxford no longer requires any additional forms, apart from the following three exceptions:

1. candidates for **choral or organ awards**
2. candidates wishing to be **interviewed overseas**
3. graduate applicants for the **accelerated medical course**.

Step five: submitting written work

Another way in which admissions tutors decide whether or not to interview you – if you are applying for an essay-based subject – is by looking at a sample of your written work. This is something that you need to consider once you have submitted your application form(s). By looking at one of your essays, the admissions tutors will be able to assess your ability to research, organise information, form opinions and construct a coherent and cogent argument in writing. These are essential skills to have when studying an essay subject at Oxbridge, and the admissions tutors need to see that you have these skills, and the potential to improve.

Normally the essay that you send will have been written as part of your A level course. Make sure that you send a particularly good example of your work; ask your teachers to suggest changes and then to re-mark the essay when you have improved it as much as possible.

Do not, however, submit anything that could not have been written by you. Plagiarism will be very obvious to admissions tutors and could potentially get you into some tricky situations at interview, since submitted written work is often discussed then.

> *'The submitted essay is often used as the starting point for discussion in the interview. The essay can show us whether the candidate has the ability to argue and has academic confidence.'*
> Admissions Tutor, Cambridge

At Cambridge, each college has a different policy on written work, but you are more likely to be asked to send in work if you are applying to read an arts or social sciences subject. The college will contact you directly if it requires work from you.

The Oxford prospectus gives clear instructions about what you need to send and when. Remember to inform your teachers in advance that you will need to send marked work.

If you have applied to Oxford, you will need to submit marked work for the following subjects (www.ox.ac.uk/admissions/undergraduate/applying-to-oxford/written-work):

- archaeology and anthropology
- classical archaeology and ancient history
- classics
- classics and English
- classics and modern languages
- classics and oriental studies
- English and modern languages
- English language and literature
- European and Middle Eastern languages
- fine art (portfolio submission)
- history
- history (ancient and modern)
- history and economics
- history and English

- history and modern languages
- history and politics
- history of art
- modern languages
- modern languages and linguistics
- music
- oriental studies
- philosophy and modern languages
- philosophy and theology
- theology and religion
- theology and oriental studies.

Step six: await the call for interview!

See Chapter 9 for more advice on interviews.

How to write your personal statement

This part of the application process can be tortuous if you allow yourself to overcomplicate matters. The quest for the 'perfect personal statement' is like searching for the Holy Grail. There's no such thing; or, if there is, you will have died of exhaustion before you find it.

You might want to remind yourself before you start of what admissions tutors are looking for.

> 'Cambridge is looking for very capable students, academically. It has to be selective as there is such stiff competition for places. On average, there are six applicants per place per year. Cambridge works its students very hard once they are here, so students need to be able to keep up with the pace and intensity. Cambridge wants motivated and committed students. Students need to spend time in the library and time thinking about their subject, so they need to be self-disciplined, well-organised and independent in their approach to their studies. Students need to be really interested in their subject. The advice is to pick a subject you really like and that you will really enjoy studying. Students should think carefully before choosing a subject.

> 'Oxford and Cambridge will look at prior grades. Good grades at AS are the best indicator of how students will perform. Regarding the personal statement, students should write about why they have chosen their subject and what they have found out about their subject outside school, such as research, public lectures, wider reading and work experience if applicable. Interviews are usually subject-based and problem-solving. Oxford and Cambridge

want to see how students can work things out, how they think and whether they can work on their own.

'As part of their preparation for an Oxford or Cambridge application, students should work hard. They should do as well as they can in their AS examinations, as they will need good grades. They should carry out independent research into their subjects. Finally, they should practise talking about ideas.

'With specific regard to international students, they need Band 7.5 in IELTS overall, with 7 in every component. By the time of the interview, applicants would need to be operating at Band 6, in order to be able to cope with the interview. International students should work especially hard on improving their English.'
Admissions Department, Sidney Sussex College, Cambridge

Think of things from the admissions tutor's point of view. What constitutes a great personal statement as far as they're concerned? Most candidates will present themselves with excellent grades, predicted or actual, and glowing references from their teachers. They may also have taken specific admission tests or submitted written work. The personal statement is one more element that the staff can use to judge whether or not a candidate will be suitable for their courses. Most admissions tutors are keen to stress that all candidates' applications are viewed 'in the round'. Be assured that they are not expecting your personal statement to be a literary masterpiece or a work of stunning originality. They want to hear about you, and, in particular:

- what interests you about your chosen subject (and why)
- why you want to study the subject(s) you've applied for
- what you have learned or done outside your college or school syllabus
- which activities you've participated in that have added to your knowledge of your subject
- what you do apart from studying and why this is important to you, especially if it relates to your subject
- what you hope to do after you've finished university, if you currently have an idea.

How to get started — some dos and don'ts

Do take time to submit something that is well written; i.e. the grammar and spelling should be correct, and you should write in sentences rather than a list. Ask your teacher or someone you trust to read it through carefully for mistakes.

Do go into detail. It's better to write in detail about a few topics than try to cite lots of interesting topics in a cursory way. Use examples to demonstrate your understanding of your subject so far and your desire to explore your subject further.

Do justify everything that you put down on paper. 'I found going to lectures at the LSE fascinating' only begs the question 'Why?'

Don't be tempted to just list the books that you have read; explain how reading them enriched your learning or excited you and made you want to read around your subject. Similarly, please don't tell them that you've read the obvious choices; when the twentieth economics applicant says that they've enjoyed *Freakonomics*, even the most well-disposed tutor will marvel at a student's lack of imagination.

Don't use long, convoluted sentences that are hard to follow; the admissions tutor may lose concentration before he or she reaches the end of the paragraph. Your writing should be clear, concise and precise.

Don't lie; you will be found out. If you are lucky enough to be called for interview you will be asked about your personal statement, and although you may not remember that you said that you read and enjoyed Nietzsche's *Twilight of the Idols*, the tutor interviewing you will. Be warned!

Don't be tempted to spend too much time listing your achievements outside school. No more than a quarter of your personal statement should be devoted to non-academic matters. Always try to demonstrate the relevance of your outside experience to your chosen subject; some of it may not be directly relevant but you are likely to have acquired useful, transferable skills that can be highlighted.

Another important consideration is the fact that your personal statement needs to be no more than 47 lines or 4,000 characters including spaces; this is a strict limit and so you need to ensure that you are as close to this as possible.

Many schools who are very successful at getting their students into Oxbridge adopt a fairly formulaic approach to writing personal statements. This is certainly one way of making your life a little easier and it might help you on your first draft. But remember, the key to writing your personal statement is that it should be personal; if you allow lots of people to read yours, you will receive lots of different opinions on its strengths and weaknesses. This can be confusing, to say the least. In the end, the best advice is to decide what you want to say and say it with conviction, in your own words, not those of your parents, teachers or other advisers. A typical personal statement takes time and effort to get right; don't expect perfection after one draft.

A model Oxbridge personal statement

There are no hard and fast rules about how to structure your personal statement. Below, however, is an example of how a well-organised statement might be written, with a synopsis, paragraph by paragraph. Below each synopsis is an example of a paragraph written by a candidate who did get a place at Oxford to study history and ancient history. Read the example carefully, but **do not copy it**.

The **first paragraph** should explain what sparked your interest in your chosen subject and why you wish to study it at university.

> My passion for history and ancient history began, perhaps unusually, in the genre of historical novels, and the more general histories of those such as Norwich and Goldsworthy. These originally caught my imagination with their sweeping narratives of the Roman military world, and the world of late antiquity. This swiftly sparked an interest in more specific and more scholarly works, such as Syme's 'The Roman Revolution', which made me think differently about my assumptions of the power of individuals; in this case Augustus' role as the product of a talented new ruling class, rather than as a lone genius, as well as Scullard's 'From the Gracchi to Nero', on the challenges which Rome faced internally, as she externally became a superpower, and the necessary changes which the fall of the republic would later bring about.

In **paragraph two** you could discuss your particular interests in relation to your university subject choice. This is your chance to write about specific ideas you have developed as a result of reading beyond your A level syllabus.

> What perhaps fascinates me the most is the way in which history, particularly in the distant past, is perceived by the succeeding generations of scholars, either through a difference of opinion in scholarly debate, or as a natural result of their environment. For example, Gibbon's demonisation of the Byzantine Empire, despite hardly being based in historical fact, is easy to understand in the context of the founding of the European world empires and the Enlightenment. Another example of this is the illusion of the founding of nations during the dark ages, and the tendency of historians to link the kingdoms of the dark ages with the modern states they were to form later on. Christopher Wickham's discussion of this phenomenon, in his 'The Inheritance of Rome', interested me immensely, as it made me question the blind belief which I had shown before when reading the narrative history of this period. Perhaps in a less orthodox way, I was also heavily influenced by Terry Jones' protestations at the misinterpretation of Celtic culture in his study 'Barbarians'. Though clearly it is difficult to make assertions about an empire without trusting your sources to some degree, it is nevertheless hugely interesting to read history from a contrary viewpoint.

The **third paragraph** can start to incorporate your personal experiences and how these have shaped your academic interests and choice of university subject.

> Another stimulating part of studying both history and ancient history is the way in which one can see how different cultures have left their mark on a particular place. A good example of this, particularly in an ancient context, is in Tunisia, where the Phoenicians, the Carthaginians, the Romans, the Vandals, the Byzantines and the Arabs have all left their mark in the numerous sites, which are fascinating in the context of both ancient and modern history. To follow this up, therefore, independently, I have done a week-long trip, in which I did a route involving retracing Cato's last march, as well as looking at the ruins of Jugurtha's capital at Beja, which has since seen many conquerors, the Byzantine fortress at Kelibia, the remarkable Arabic city of Kairouan, and the Roman ruins at Dougga. One piece of extended work which I have done this summer has been on the Jugurthine war, and the other was on Justinian's capture of Africa from the Vandals. I have also used my trip to supplement my research, as well as to develop much further my knowledge of post-Almohad Tunisian history.

The **fourth paragraph** can include a brief summary of your extracurricular activities. Remember, the admissions tutor will have to live with you for three years if you get in to his or her college. You need to come across as a responsible, interesting person who will be an asset to the college.

> Outside of the academic sphere, my main passion is music. I play the double bass to grade seven standard, and have recently started the jazz double bass, as well as enjoying collecting vinyl records. I have also attended many Model United Nations meetings, which I have enjoyed and have excelled in, particularly those set in historical situations. I am also interested in journalism, in which I have done work experience, and I would hope to contribute to magazines at university. My reading, though mostly focused on history, also encompasses literature, and I am particularly interested in the great American novel, having been moved by the work of Fitzgerald, Hemingway and Capote, as well as the works of Leo Tolstoy, Maxim Gorky, and Fyodor Dostoevsky.

Examples of successful Oxbridge personal statements

While researching this book, I spoke to many students in order to find out what they had found most helpful when they were applying to Oxford and Cambridge. Without question, the most useful thing given to these students seemed to be examples of really good personal statements.

What follows, therefore, is a raft of excellent personal statements collected over recent years. It is important to stress that it's worth reading not just the one specific to your subject. I hope that you can see several common factors that have impressed Oxbridge tutors.

- They explain clearly why the student wants to study the subject that they have applied for.
- They are well written; there are no spelling mistakes or grammatical errors.
- They show that the candidate has the ability to think logically, critically and independently.
- They show enthusiasm and clear motivation through their detailed examples of how the student has explored their subject beyond the A level syllabus – by extra reading, through work experience or through attendance on extracurricular courses.
- They show that the student has the skills necessary for studying at a university where the tutorial system reigns; that they are organised, committed and able to put forward a point of view and justify it.
- They show that the candidate is the sort of person the tutors would like to teach.
- If the student has gap-year plans, they relate them to the chosen area of study.

It is a useful exercise once you have finished a first draft to see how many of these qualities your personal statement encompasses.

Economics - Cambridge (3,977 characters, with spaces)

I come from Zhejiang, a coastal province located in the east of China, one of the most commercial and affluent Chinese provinces. It is hard to conceive that not long ago there were no televisions or telephones, and residents used food stamps to purchase necessities of life which were granted and limited by the central government. Due to reforms introduced by Deng Xiaoping, who served as the 'paramount leader' of the People's Republic of China from 1978 to 1992, Zhejiang flourished from a poor village to a commercial hub. Deng introduced capitalist market principles involving privatisation of agriculture and opened up the country to foreign investment. Learning about this development was the first time I was attracted to the power of macroeconomic mechanisms.

During my A level studies I further discovered the power of economics through the course content and reading around my subjects. 'The Return of Depression Economics and the Crisis of 2008' by Paul Krugman discusses several depressions and each government's economic policies in reaction to them. Due to the fact that most economic concepts predict what is likely to happen, holding a basic assumption that people are rational, all the dogmas become muddled in times of economic and social crisis because individuals' minds are unpredictable. Within this book, the explanation of Japan's economy bubble in the 1980s led me to establish links with recent conditions in China as China may suffer from a 'growth recession' as well. It is striking to consider the future of China's economic position; because of its political system and economic policies, the outcome is unpredictable. Also, reading 'Globalisation and its Discontents' highlighted the fault of international institutions in the process of globalisation, especially of the IMF.

My academic capabilities provide me with a solid foundation for studying economics. Through studying maths and further maths at A level, and being awarded a gold medal in the Maths Challenge, I possess a strong mathematical background. I am keen to apply my analytical techniques and problem solving skills in new areas, such as game theory using the mathematical approaches to observe economic activity. Studying economics has provided me with an overview of the world economy. The key definitions, models and theories have enabled me to understand and digest current affairs. As an international student, I have studied some Chinese political and economic policies; there is no doubt that my background would offer me an expansive horizon to study economics.

Outside my academic studies, I have gained work experience in the Industrial and Commercial Bank of China. I was based in the marketing department where I discovered the fundamental concepts of international trade. For instance, I learned that a Letter of Credit is the major method of payment in international trade. I also experienced the non-cash counter; the bank clerk showed me the process of Project Eight Remittance which is informed by a collection of codes. This experience enabled me to gain professional knowledge first hand. It was interesting to see aspects of my studies being used in a working business environment. I have always enjoyed trying new things, and moving from China to England allowed me to challenge myself even further. I am a member of the Student Council, which has provided me with the opportunity to voice my opinions, discuss key points with my peers and meet a wider range of people. Outside my studies, I am passionate about history and political issues. Gaining an insight into these has made me critically and logically aware and able to appreciate different perspectives.

I look forward to furthering my knowledge at university and beyond. The knowledge I aspire to cultivate is essential for modern living, the way economists think about and analyse problems in a logical way is applicable to so many areas and will furnish me with numerous opportunities for the future.

English – Cambridge: character count (with spaces) 3,980

The prospect of reading English at university excites me a great deal – learning to see and to see differently, with fresh eyes and new apparatus for understanding. Arriving at Imagism and Ezra Pound through my study of W. B. Yeats, I became captivated by some of Pound's shorter poems, found in 'Personae', particularly 'In a Station of the Metro'. I found that I was particularly interested in how Pound's laconic phrasing facilitates a direct correspondence between images and words, especially the way his poem works like a series of sense impressions, constructing a moment of Modernist beauty which is passing, fragmentary and attached to something lost. Formed in relation to the Japanese hokku, Pound's poem and others like it attempt to 'record the precise instant when a thing outward and objective transforms itself, or darts into a thing inward and subjective'. This movement that he describes, almost ineffable, specifies the point at which literature shatters its structure and takes on a sense of humanity, where perhaps it is its most affecting.

In my experience, literature acts as a kind of memory, and the most powerful memories we have are those most vivid to us; resonant, clear; even sonorous. Reading Roland Barthes' book, 'Camera Lucida', which examines presence and absence in photography, I was prompted to consider the way Barthes confronts his sense of loss to establish the theoretical idea of 'punctum' – the wounding detail of a photograph. In Samuel Beckett's 'Krapp's Last Tape', Krapp listens repeatedly to a passage of tape that contains a memory of love lost. He lingers upon this moment, affected by its contents and the fondness in his voice. It is a moment of punctum in literature, a particularly rare instance of affection in the work of Beckett, and one tinged with longing, only accentuated by an ailing Harold Pinter's stark performance of the character in 2006.

Shakespeare's tragedy 'King Lear' sees characters blinded, in the dark and forced to fashion a way. Close to death and removed of their comfort, the parallel protagonists of the play, Lear and Gloucester, are made to – as Wallace Stevens writes in his poem 'The Snow Man' – understand the 'nothing that is not ... and the nothing that is'. Through its brutal collision of matter and nothingness, what the play foregrounds is a pursuit of authentic selfhood: Lear's search is for the phrase 'As I am a man', and upon voicing it, Shakespeare's character makes a simple, beautiful acknowledgment. This elusive sense of being 'close to life' is arguably the primary concern of Virginia Woolf's writing, her aim being a literature that offers the true reality of human experience. In her novel 'To The Lighthouse', reality is written with intricacy and depth, consciousness running from one thing to another. Woolf's craft is to survey the infinitesimal; she then stretches out time, moving from paint-strokes to seasons, achieving the intimate and the sublime. What Woolf's ever more experimental method allowed her to achieve was a more complete picture of physical and psychological narrative, and I am interested in considering how her experimentation fits into the wider canon, what T. S. Eliot called 'the present moment of the past', 'a living whole of all ... that has ever been written'.

My work as editorial assistant at the White Review and Acme Paper over the past year has not only afforded me the chance to handle fiction, poetry and essays, but has also served to broaden my appreciation of contemporary writing by leading to my discovery of authors and poets such as Laszlo Krasznahorkai and John Ashbery. During my gap year I intend to travel to East Asia and I am excited to explore the literature and ideas of another place. A consequence of my practice as a photographer, and having studied history of art, my engagement with literature has been informed by a consideration of images and imagery, and I look forward to further investigating their relationship in my studies.

Computer Science - Cambridge (3,899 characters, with spaces)

The logical approach to solving complicated problems is the main driving force behind my enjoyment of computing and programming. For me one of the stimulating challenges of computer science is searching for ways to optimise my solutions to problems.

Computing has many practical uses, leading to a variety of personally fascinating fields such as artificial intelligence and software engineering, while computational physics and robotics appeal to my interest in physics and computer science combined. Recently, reading 'The New Turing Omnibus' has introduced me to even more areas of computer science. I have enjoyed reading chapters on detecting prime numbers and program correctness. Furthermore, topics such as binary search trees and the Newton-Raphson method have encouraged me to write my own related programs.

Whilst studying at Allameh Helli School, computing was a large part of my core syllabus. There I learnt programming in various languages including C and C++. At every opportunity I took part in the extra computing classes offered, which included topics such as algorithms for data manipulation, computer graphics for games programming, object-oriented programming and computational simulations. My greatest achievement was playing a key role on the 3D soccer simulation project. Our team qualified for the 2012 Dutch Open and Iran Open robotics competitions, even though many university teams did not manage to qualify. This project allowed me to combine my interest in both physics and computing by challenging my ability to produce specific algorithms and programs based on my knowledge of physics and mechanics. Prior to this, my Chemical Clock project won 2nd place in the National Young Researcher's competition in middle school. During my AS year I completed my Mathematics A level and took part in the UK Mathematics Trust's Senior Challenge, securing a gold certificate. This year I am completing A levels in Further Maths, Physics and Economics.

Recently, my knowledge of mathematical algebra proved useful in understanding a paper I read in the 'Communications of the ACM' magazine describing different cake-cutting algorithms. It interestingly went on to explain how these algorithms could help solve real issues such as the equitable division of limited natural resources. In economics, it was intriguing to learn how firms such as Hyde Park Global Investments use computer technology to meet their objectives. This firm uses computers instead of hedge fund managers to buy and sell shares, as being a nanosecond faster than their rivals equates to profits of tens of thousands of pounds. My knowledge of physics has proved invaluable when writing programs. For example, I am currently studying about projectiles in mechanics, which goes perfectly hand in hand with the work I carried out in middle school, creating simulations of freefall and other physics experiments.

I have always brought commitment and enthusiasm to every aspect of my school life. At my previous school I was part of the organisational committee for our science and technology seminars. I was also in charge of organising the first games programming competition between schools at a national level. Whilst being a scholarship student at MPW, I have been appointed as a mentor to international students and elected onto the student council. I am part of the school's debating team and have successfully participated in the Debating Matters public speaking competition. Beyond academics I enjoy playing sports such as football and volleyball. These experiences have strengthened my independence, leadership and teamwork skills, which will help my transition into university education. I believe that my strong ability for logical reasoning and problem solving combined with passion and commitment to the subject offer the prerequisite needed to succeed as an undergraduate computer scientist.

History of Art - Oxford (3,927 characters, with spaces)

As a Malaysian, I was exposed at an early age to an abundant variety of art, diverse yet interconnected in style and technique. Having lived in Asia, I had the chance to visit neighbouring countries and see the Caves of the Thousand Buddhas along the Silk Road in China, as well as the Angkor Wat in Cambodia. I also visited the World Expo in Shanghai, which was one of the greatest experiences of my life. The visually fascinating UK Pavilion (otherwise known as the 'Seed Cathedral') and the Spain Pavilion particularly caught my attention. Despite their obvious architectural differences – UK with its 60,000 fibre optic rods and Spain with its remarkable wickerwork façade – they both presented the same underlying idea which was sustainability. My travels and experiences throughout the years have stimulated my interest in the history of art.

To get a better insight into art history, I read 'The Story of Art' by Gombrich and then proceeded to study classical myths and religion. I have visited world-renowned museums such as the Louvre in Paris, the Rijksmuseum in Amsterdam and the National Gallery in London. I particularly enjoy Renaissance art, but also find modern art very refreshing: visiting Kazimir Malevich's Tate Modern exhibition led me to an article about Malevich's Red House by Tom Lubbock; it enabled me to look beyond the abstract and the ordinary, changing the way I perceived suprematism and contemporary art as a whole. On the other hand, my visit to the Sensing Spaces Exhibition at the Royal Academy of Arts taught me how an architecture and spatial design can affect the atmosphere and evoke emotions through physical perception.

As a part of the Gifted and Talented Group for English Literature and having studied Biology at AS Level, I have gained invaluable critical and analytical skills. I became aware of the influences of science and literature on art; for example, how the dissection of the human body led to Leonardo da Vinci's success in his faithful imitations of life and how the Victorian ballad 'The Lady of Shalott' inspired J. W. Waterhouse's painting of the same name. I read King Lear, and watched it performed at the National Theatre in London. This prompted me to look at James Barry's painting, King Lear Weeping over the Dead Body of Cordelia, displayed at Tate Britain. Despite the story being told through different mediums and set on different timelines, both play and painting evoked emotions as raw and forlorn as the other. To further immerse myself in the subject, I will be taking a one-year AS/A2 History of Art course starting in September 2014. Richard Stemp's book 'The Secret Language of the Renaissance' was a stepping stone for me; and the prospect of learning more about how to read paintings, sculpture and architecture excites me, especially the opportunity to understand how art reflects society.

With my experience as the secretary of my school's Craft Club, I learned administrative skills as well as the importance of good communication. These skills helped my team win the Special Prize in the Edible Architecture Competition. Predating Stonehenge by 6000 years, the Göbekli Tepe of Turkey became one of the main inspirations for this project. The structure that we built was to be a sacred temple surrounded by the sea; it comprised of two circular enclosures and five Solomonic columns – much like the ones in Raphael's cartoon, the Healing of the Lame Man – supporting a sugar glass dome. Furthermore, I will be competing for the ARTiculation Prize 2015 to develop my confidence and ability to express my thoughts and appreciation for art.

As a creative and inquisitive student, I am constantly driven by challenges and new experiences. The study of art history will not only be exciting, it will also provide me with a great foundation for a successful career in teaching so that I may one day be able to share my enthusiasm and knowledge with others.

Economics and Management – Oxford (3,988 characters, with spaces)

I am stimulated by the ever-changing nature of management, particularly the way different disciplines of management are combined to respond to economic conditions. I studied business management, accounting and economics for two years in Australia. Since then, real-life observations of A level Economics concepts, such as the division of labour, and their links to management, have furthered my desire to specialise in the subjects.

Having lived in three different countries, my cross-cultural experience led to my interest in the running of the global economy and how it can affect individual firms. I researched by reading Stiglitz's 'Globalisation and Its Discontents', which I found relevant to the issue of Vietnam's accession to the WTO not meeting expectations. I looked into rent-seeking, recalling how my father, a businessman, complained about the corruption and red tape that fostered uncertainty in his business activities. While Stiglitz argues that rapid privatisation, which Vietnam is pursuing, will only lead to more corruption, Professor John Kay, in his LSE lecture on 'The Future of Capitalism', believes that this transition to the market economy will keep rent-seeking in check. I explored this complexity about political economy briefly in Wolff's 'An Introduction to Political Philosophy'. Also, Stiglitz's account of the negative transition of the Soviet Union to a capitalist state provides an interesting comparison with my research in Vietnam, a communist state, a topic which I would like to elaborate further at degree level.

In July, I worked as an intern at Eximland, a property investment firm in Ho Chi Minh City. I gained first-hand understanding of diversification and strategic management. The firm responded to the frozen property market in the last 3 years by turning an apartment and office building project into a retreat facility for a nearby hospital. I did work experience at Fimex Saota Co, a large seafood export firm in South Vietnam. At the firm's factories, dominated by women, the monotony of specialisation was apparent. This interests me in studying the aspects of organisational behaviour, such as workplace diversity or job satisfaction. I was already intrigued by the discussion of the controversies and job satisfaction, the 'tournament theory' and the corporate environment, where performance pay doesn't always increase productivity, in Harford's 'The Logic of Life'.

Studying philosophy and art history gives me clarity and coherence in written communication. I discovered interesting links between the subjects, such as Thompson's 'The 12 Million

Stuffed-shark'. It discusses how the contemporary art market is dictated by branding and involves theories such as the Veblen effect, where Chinese businessmen buy Western art as displays of status. In the Renaissance, the Medici family in Florence also commissioned great works of art to gain respect. From 'commodified' art to art being used as another currency by investors or the effect of the increasingly inelastic supply of the traditional art market on the demand for contemporary art, the book shows me how economics and management can be applied to a wide range of industries.

I had two part-time jobs, as a tutor and a coffee barista, in Australia. This honed my ability to work effectively under pressure. Living in London, I like to cycle and visit galleries and exhibitions. In June, I set up a project in Vietnam to sell cakes at a children's theatre to raise funds for charity. It allows me to practise my knowledge of market research and financial strategy as well as my skills of problem solving and team work. I achieved a distinction in the Australian Economics Competition and was team leader in the Edith Cowan University's Business Experience and the ASX Sharemarket Game. I am participating in this year's Target 2.0 Competition to challenge myself further. I believe my experience and background have made me an adaptive, open-minded and unique individual.

Economics — Cambridge: character count (including spaces) 3,676

I have observed rapid economic growth in my hometown Guangzhou, such as a noticeable improvement in the quality of commodities. Exploring the main forces behind this development has inspired me to continue to study economics, and try to enhance my understanding of how China and the whole world operates. During my A level studies, I have also found that mathematics helps me to explain economic behaviour through simplified models, enabling conclusions to be deduced logically. I am eager to discover more about the interplay of both disciplines in my future studies.

I am intrigued by microeconomics as it provides an insight into how markets work, and enables me to explain economic phenomena in real-life scenarios. Recently, the launch of the new iPhone triggered a price competition between Telecom and Unicom, two phone operators in China. I observed that this event stimulated large demand in the market and the changes of revenue for these companies closely follow the theory of price elasticity of demand. We benefit from lower prices as consumer surplus has increased, but I realised that our welfare can be damaged as the quality of the products may be sacrificed. As a result of my interest in this price war, I studied it further and found game theory can help to analyse it. To gain additional insight, I listened to a lecture online given by Ben Polak about five basic conclusions of game theory and learnt that rational choices can lead to bad outcomes. For example, the colour television industry in China exited the market as a result of declining profits although a firm may be better to reduce prices in response to a price war initiated by the other. I started reading 'Thinking Strategically' by Avinash Dixit, and understood how the Nash equilibrium is obtained and can be utilised to explain the reactions of Unicom and Telecom. I discovered that mathematical methods are widely applied in game theory such as using probabilities to calculate the expected payoffs.

I am always curious about the reasoning behind mathematical principles such as the proof of the sum of squares formula. After reading 'Mathematics: A Very Short Introduction' by Timothy Gowers, I engaged in proving that the square root of two is an irrational number, and appreciated how mathematicians approach and solve problems. I learnt to apply maths to economics and use differentiation to find the profit maximisation of a firm. Another branch of maths I enjoy is statistics, as it makes me work rigorously not only in dealing with many numbers but also in other subjects. I studied the statistical methods applied in economics such as using regression analysis to show negative correlations between any country's GDP and its unemployment rate. Learning Olympiad maths from a young age has also improved my logical thinking and problem-solving skills.

I was pleased to do an internship at the Bank of China and witness how some banks in China suffer from financial problems. This experience enhanced my communication skills and enabled me to see how economic theories actually apply in the real world such as increasing interest rates in order to attract more savings. Participating in the Bank of England competition has given me broader knowledge and skills of teamwork. I have gained a method of explaining concepts more briefly from helping my classmates study. I enjoy playing piano and have achieved grade 8, demonstrating my strong discipline and perseverance.

I relish new theories and methods and enjoy the satisfaction obtained from thinking and working out complex problems. A hard-working attitude and determination will help equip me to face the challenges of university.

The UCAS application

These are the steps you need to take, and when to take them, to apply through UCAS.

1. Go to www.ucas.com/students/apply/undergraduate to register in September. In order to do this you will need an email address. If you have a school email address, use it to register; if you haven't got a school email address, go to www.yahoo.com or www.hotmail.com and get a free one. When you register on the UCAS website, you will be sent an application number, user name and password, which you will need every time you log on to the UCAS website.
2. The entire application is done online. Although it may seem complex and time consuming, you can complete it in stages and come back to it. There are 'help' sections all the way through the form in case you get stuck.
3. Fill in the 'Personal details' section, which includes your name, address and date of birth.
4. Fill in the 'Student support' section, which is where you have to select your fee code. If you are a British national your local authority will be your fee payer.
5. Next is an 'Additional information' section in which you can list the activities you have done in preparation for further education. These activities specifically refer to attending summer schools in preparation for university, run by either the universities themselves or trusts such as the Sutton Trust. See www.suttontrust.com/home or contact UCAS for more information (www.ucas.com/about_us/contact_us).
6. The next section is where you enter your university choices. You can apply to either Oxford or Cambridge. Choose the correct university code from the drop-down menu (CAM C05 for Cambridge or OXF O33 for Oxford. You also need to add what UCAS calls the 'campus code', which is the college code. A drop-down list will appear again. You will also need to choose the subject and select which year of entry you are applying for.
7. The next section asks you for details of your education. You need to write down every GCSE and A level (or equivalent qualification) you have taken and what grade you got under the heading of the school in which you took them. If you are applying post-A level, you need to write down all of your module grades.
8. The next section is 'Employment'. This does not ask you about work experience but about paid employment. It is worth writing down even the most insignificant jobs you have done – washing dishes at the local restaurant, for example – since admissions tutors will value the commitment and maturity you will have shown when holding down a job.
9. Next is the 'Personal statement'. This is your chance to show the admissions tutors how you write and how informed you are about

your subject. You should write this in a Word document, spell check it and read it through carefully, then, when it is ready, copy and paste it into the UCAS form.

10. Finally, send the application in the first week of October to be completed by your teachers. In order to do this, you have to pay £22 (or £11 if you are applying to just one university) to UCAS to process your information. This must be paid by credit card (your school may have a policy of paying this for you so you need to check before you part with any money). Your teacher will then be able to open your application on the teachers' part of the UCAS site. They will read it to check everything is correct and will then write their reference and your predicted grades. Your teacher may need some time to write the reference, so do make sure you have your part done well in advance.

11. Your teacher then needs to submit your UCAS application by 6p.m. on **15 October**.

8 | Succeeding in written tests

Over the past few years, more and more students are achieving As and A*s at A level. As it has become harder to identify academically outstanding students through their A level results, both Oxford and Cambridge now rely on additional testing systems when selecting candidates for interview. The following chapter aims to give an account of the various written tests students face prior to or during their interviews, including the deadlines for registering for the exams; when and where the tests are sat; details about the structure of the tests, including knowledge requirements; sample questions; and useful links for more information and practice.

These tests include the BMAT for medicine and the LNAT for law at Oxford, two externally administered tests. The History Aptitude Test (HAT) is taken for history at Oxford and there are various similar but internal exams set by Cambridge colleges. Sixth Term Examination Papers (STEP) have been reintroduced for maths at Cambridge as well as the Thinking Skills Assessment (TSA) for various other Oxford and Cambridge subjects. These exams aim to highlight the natural intelligence and academic potential of the candidate and, in doing so, widen access. Since it is often difficult to revise for the Oxbridge written tests, students have to rely on their innate intellectual ability to complete them. In theory, students whose schools have provided less preparation should not be disadvantaged.

The style of testing also differs from what many school leavers will be used to. Whereas A levels often test factual recall, the Oxbridge written exams look for analytical and critical capabilities. It should be noted, therefore, that these tests are likely to be much harder than anything you will have experienced at school. This is taken into consideration, and admissions tutors do not expect students to achieve 100%.

Oxford and Cambridge take different approaches to additional written tests in some subjects. Oxford exams are standardised: for example, all students applying for history across the whole university will take exactly the same test (the HAT). In contrast, Cambridge tests vary from college to college.

- www.medsci.ox.ac.uk/study/medicine/pre-clinical/requirements
- www.lnat.ac.uk
- www.ox.ac.uk/admissions/undergraduate/applying-to-oxford/tests
- www.history.ox.ac.uk/prospective/undergraduate/applying/the-history-aptitude-test.html
- www.admissionstestingservice.org/for-test-takers/step/about-step
- www.study.cam.ac.uk/undergraduate/apply/tests/bmat.html
- www.admissionstestingservice.org/for-test-takers/thinking-skills-assessment/tsa-oxford/about-tsa-oxford
- www.admissionstestingservice.org/for-test-takers/thinking-skills-assessment/tsa-cambridge/about-tsa-cambridge

Testing happens at various stages during the application process. Some tests are sat in early November at your school. The results of these tests can then play a part in determining whether you are called to interview. Some tests – including the majority of those for Cambridge – take place when you go up for interview in early December. The results are then used, alongside your interview performance, your personal statement, your school references and your exam grades, to decide whether you should be made a conditional offer.

Don't let taking these tests put you off applying. If you are serious about wanting a place at a top university, you should be able to do well without masses of additional tuition or extra work. It is very important, however, to go online and get full details of what the tests entail and to do some practice papers if they are offered.

Oxford admissions tests

The schedule of tests for 2015 entry is as shown below.

1 October 2015

- This is the usual deadline date for registering for the BMAT, although the actual date had not been confirmed at the time of writing this guide.

15 October 2015

- This is the usual final deadline for registering for the BMAT, the English Literature Admissions Test (ELAT), the HAT, the Physics Aptitude Test (PAT) and the TSA, although the date had yet to be confirmed at the time of writing.
- Closing date for all UCAS applications to Oxford and Cambridge
- Closing date for receipt of applications for the accelerated medical course

September–October 2015

- LNAT

November 2015 (usually midweek in the first week, although this had yet to be confirmed at time of writing)

- BMAT
- ELAT
- HAT
- PAT
- Aptitude Test for Mathematics and Computer Science
- TSA
- Tests for all modern languages courses
- Tests for all classics courses

Cambridge admissions tests

Thinking Skills Assessment

You may be required to sit the Cambridge TSA, either online or on paper, when you attend your interview. This test examines critical thinking and problem-solving skills and is used by some colleges for these courses:

- computer science
- economics
- engineering
- human, social and political sciences
- land economy
- natural sciences.

It is not necessary to register in advance for the TSA (Cambridge) and there is no fee for it. The college to which you have applied will inform you about the details of the test, if you have to take it.

Biomedical Assessment Test

All medicine and veterinary medicine applicants must sit the BMAT after they have submitted their application and before they have their set interview date. The test examines scientific aptitude and concentrates on the requisite skills needed for studying medicine and veterinary medicine.

The BMAT is also used by some other universities for medical and dental applicants.

Applicants are responsible for ensuring that they enter for the BMAT by 1 October 2015. The BMAT test will usually be in the first week of November 2015. The final dates should appear on the BMAT website in the spring of 2015.

There is a cost for the BMAT, details of which may be found on the BMAT website (www.admissiontestingservice.org/our-services/medicine-and-healthcare/bmat). Certain UK candidates who receive financial support may apply for their BMAT fees to be refunded. Such applicants should get in touch with the BMAT support team for further information.

Cambridge Law Test

Most Cambridge Law applicants are required to sit the Cambridge Law Test, which is designed to assess candidates' suitability for the Cambridge law degree.

The test is taken at interview. Applicants who are interviewed overseas sit a slightly different version of the test (see the Faculty of Law website, www.law.cam.ac.uk, for details). No prior knowledge of the law is required or expected. You don't need to register in advance – your college will contact you about the arrangements – and there's no charge associated with taking the Cambridge Law Test.

Although these tests cannot be revised for it is advisable to make sure you know what to expect and practise the tests beforehand. Information on BMAT can be found at www.admissionstestingservice.org/for-test-takers/bmat/about-bmat and follow the links to find specimen papers. For further information about how the universities view and use the tests can be found on their own websites (www.medsci.ox.ac.uk/study/medicine/pre-clinical/faqs/bmat-gcses-and-short-listing/what-is-the-bmat and www.study.cam.ac.uk/undergraduate/apply/tests/bmat.html).

For information on TSA Oxford and TSA Cambridge go to www.admissionstestingservice.org/for-test-takers/thinking-skills-assessment and follow the links for the appropriate institution and test. There are also specimen papers here.

Information on LNAT can be found at www.lnat.ac.uk with practice tests at http://lnat.dev3.oneltd.eu/how-to-prepare/practice-test.

Information on HAT and specimen papers can be found at www.history.ox.ac.uk/prospective/undergraduate/applying/the-history-aptitude-test.html.

For information on ELAT go to www.admissionstestingservice.org/for-test-takers/elat and follow the links on the site to find further details of the test and specimen papers.

Some tips for taking specialist tests

- Remember that Oxford and Cambridge have designed these tests to try to give them another tool to differentiate between students. They are looking for those who are most academically suited to their courses. You should not need to spend hours preparing to take these tests; in fact, if you need to undertake an enormous amount of preparation, it is arguable that you may not be an appropriate candidate.
- The universities give a full description of what the specialist tests entail on their websites:
  - www.ox.ac.uk/admissions/undergraduate_courses/applying_ to_oxford/tests/index.html
  - www.study.cam.ac.uk/undergraduate/apply/tests.
- Past papers are available for all tests and it is vital that you practise some of these in mock exam conditions to familiarise yourself with the format of the tests and the time constraints on the test.
- Do not be upset if you can't answer all the questions. The tests are devised to be stretching and it is important not to panic if you come across something unfamiliar.

9 | Surviving the interview

About four to eight weeks after you have submitted your application, a letter will drop through your door. At this stage you will find out whether you have been called for interview.

If you haven't, don't despair. There's always next year or another university. It's really not the end of the world.

If you have been called for interview – congratulations! Now make the most of the opportunity presented to you and do your preparation to make the experience a positive one.

Prepare properly: the practicalities

If you live a long distance from the universities or have an exam to take, the college may ask you to stay over the night before the interview. Being in college for a night or even a few days will give you an opportunity to meet some of the current students and other candidates and, while you may find it hard to get a good night's sleep in a strange bed, you should try to make the most of the experience.

Leave plenty of time to get to your first appointment

Arrive at least half an hour earlier than you planned to. You do not want to turn up stressed and sweating. Transport links to both universities are excellent and generally reliable but it's always worth assuming the worst-case scenario and arriving with plenty of time to spare.

Print off a map

Double check that you know your college's location and make sure you have enough money to get a taxi in case you arrive late or get lost.

Have the phone number of the admissions office

Save it on your mobile and write it down (in case your battery runs out) so you can let them know if you're delayed.

Know where your interview is taking place

When you arrive and are given the location of your interview room, go and find out exactly where it is. Oxbridge colleges can be confusing to navigate around and many a candidate has arrived 10 minutes late to a 20-minute interview because they couldn't locate the right staircase. Be warned.

Dress as if you've made an effort

You don't have to wear a suit but you should look clean and not crumpled. This is not the occasion for girls to show off their cleavage, wear very short skirts or shorts, and it's probably best for both sexes to leave the football strip in the drawer. Brushing your hair is usually a good thing too. Oxbridge colleges can be cold in December (or overheated). It's best to err on the safe side and bring clothes to cover both eventualities.

Make sure you have a book, some money for food and a charged phone – it may even be worth bringing your phone charger

You may spend a lot of time waiting around. This is particularly true for Oxford interviews where you may be seen by several different colleges over a number of days. The cities are expensive and you really don't want to run out of money.

Don't relax too much!

If you meet up with friends, please don't go out and party. You will not do well at your interview the next morning and tutors will be predictably unsympathetic if you turn up the worse for wear.

Prepare properly: the interview

There's no real mystery about what you are likely to be asked at the interview. The tutors are looking for the best qualified candidates; people whom they will enjoy teaching and who will make a contribution to their academic department. It's worth reminding yourself what qualities they are looking for in a student.

> 'Keble admits about 130 students each year from all types of school and educational backgrounds to study a wide range of subjects. We seek applicants who are academically aspiring and

intellectually ambitious. We are looking for potential as much as achievement, and encourage applications from schools that do not regularly send candidates to Oxford ... We admit students on the basis of academic merit alone.'

www.keble.ox.ac.uk/admissions/undergraduate

It's essential, therefore, that you have thought through your answers to the following questions.

- Why have you applied to study your course?
- What does your course entail, all three or four years of it?
- What did you write in your personal statement and why?

When did you last read your personal statement?

You may not remember all the books that you said you had devoured but the tutor interviewing you will. You are **very** likely to be asked questions about your personal statement so take a copy with you and be sure you know what you wrote in it. The same applies to any written work and any supplementary answers that you submitted. Make sure you have copies with you and re-read them before the interview.

Do you really know your subject?

Have you read the 'Introduction to . . .' on the university and college's website? Have you read around your subject beyond the obvious choices? What else have you done that proves your interest in your subject?

Is your body language right?

During mock interviews, practise walking into a room, looking your interviewer in the eyes, smiling and saying hello and shaking their hand. Explain why you're doing this beforehand or they may be rather shocked! When you are called in to the interview room for real, try to greet your interviewers confidently even if you're feeling very nervous. Sit forward in your seat and look interested. You will score no extra points for slouching or seeming bored.

Do you know the sort of questions you may be asked?

First of all, don't worry about the apocryphal mad Oxbridge questions. Most of the questions asked will be about your A level subjects and other topics that should give you an opportunity to show your mettle. There is a list of questions below that have been asked by tutors over the past few years. It's useful to look at them to give you an idea of the type of questions that might come up, but that's all. You are much more likely to be asked a straightforward question about your subject than any of the ones on this list.

It's also important to read a decent newspaper and keep up to date with current affairs. You may be asked your opinion on something in the news, so it's definitely worth brushing up your knowledge of current affairs in preparation.

What happens if I can't answer their question?

Don't panic. There will often be no 'right' answer to whatever question you've been given. It's perfectly okay to ask for a few seconds to think about what you're going to say; something along the lines of 'That's an interesting question. Can I have a few moments to consider my answer?' makes you seem thoughtful, not desperate.

Really think through and rehearse the answers to the obvious questions to which so often even strong candidates fail to give convincing answers.

* Why do you want to read [insert subject]?
* What is it about the course that interests you? (Have you been online to ensure you know exactly what the course entails, all three or four years of it?)
* Why have you chosen [insert college name]? (Do you know the names and special interests of the tutors who will be conducting the interview? It's all there online; make sure you find out. Knowing this makes you seem well prepared and it will make you feel more confident, because you have a little inside knowledge on the people who are interviewing you.)
* Why should we give you a place to read [insert subject] rather than the nine other candidates whom we are interviewing today?

Remember, no tutor will be trying to make you feel small, trick you or humiliate you. A good interviewer will allow you to demonstrate your interest in your subject and your academic potential. They are most interested in your ability to think logically and express your ideas orally.

The big day

So the moment's finally arrived. What exactly will happen at the interview? Every experience can be different. Some colleges use a panel of interviewers, sometimes you will have consecutive interviews conducted by one individual (often the college admissions tutor, followed by one with a subject specialist) and sometimes interviewers do them in tandem.

In most cases two interviews is the standard but extra interviews may be given, or you may be sent to another college. Again, it varies.

The format will vary widely depending on subject. For some subjects (e.g. English) you may be given some prose or poetry to read before you go into your interview. You will then be asked questions on this by the tutors, who may then want to discuss the content of your personal statement – such as books you've mentioned reading or poetry you've enjoyed. For science subjects this is less common, and it is more likely that you will be given problems to solve or questions to answer. Generally these are designed to require no specific prior knowledge.

You may also be asked to attend a 'general' or 'college' interview. This is conducted by interviewers who don't teach your subject. It is possible that one of the purposes of this interview will be to see how you'll fit in with the college atmosphere and whether you are a well-rounded person who will be an asset to their college. You may be asked questions on your personal statement, about a topic of interest in the news or about your enthusiasm for your chosen subject.

Below are some examples of the sort of questions you may be asked and some students' experiences at their interviews.

General interview questions

- Why do you want to come to this college?
- What made you want to study this subject?
- What are you intending to do in your gap year?
- Where do you see yourself in five years' time?
- Excluding your A level reading, what were the last three books you read?
- What do you regard as your strengths and weaknesses?
- What extracurricular activities would you like to take part in at this college?
- Why did you make an 'open application'?
- Give us three reasons why we should offer you a place.
- What will you do if we don't offer you a place?
- Why did you choose your A level subjects?
- How will this degree help in your chosen career?
- How would your friends describe you?
- Tell us why we should accept you.
- Why have you chosen Cambridge and not Oxford (and vice versa)?

Subject-specific interview questions

Anthropology/archaeology

- Name the six major world religions.
- What does Stonehenge mean to you?

- What are the problems regarding objectivity in anthropological studies?
- Why do civilisations erect monuments?
- Why should we approach all subjects from a holistic, anthropological perspective?
- Being given an object and being told where it was found, then being asked what you could deduce from the object.
- Discussing an archaeological find.

Architecture

A large part of the interview is likely to be dedicated to discussing your portfolio. Be prepared to discuss the ideas, purposes and motivations behind your work. Your work should also illustrate a well-developed ability to relate two- and three-dimensional experience through drawing and 3D models. You should also be prepared to discuss your work experience. Below are some other questions that might be asked.

- Is architecture in decline?
- Could you describe a building that you recently found interesting?
- Do you have an architect whom you particularly admire? What is it about their work that you find attractive?
- If you could design a building anywhere in the world, and if money, space and time were unlimited, what would you design?

Art history

- What do we look for when we study art? What are we trying to reveal?
- Comment on this painting on the wall.
- Compare and contrast these three images.
- What exhibitions have you been to recently?
- How do you determine the value of art?
- Who should own art?
- What is art?
- Why is art important?
- What role do art galleries and museums play in society today?
- Are humans inherently creative?
- Apart from your studies, how else might you pursue your interest in art history while at university?
- What are some key themes in the history of art?
- How has the depiction of the human form developed through the centuries?
- Who invented linear perspective – artists or architects?
- When was the discipline of art history brought to England and by whom?

Biochemistry

- How do catalysts work?
- Describe the work of enzymes.

- Discuss the chemistry of the formation of proteins.
- Questions on oxidation, equilibria and interatomic forces.
- Questions on X-ray crystallography.
- Why do you wish to read biochemistry rather than chemistry?
- What scientific journals have you read lately? Is there a recent development in the field that particularly interests you?
- Why does most biochemistry take place away from equilibrium? (Or, how important is equilibrium to biochemical processes?)

Biological sciences

- How does the immune system recognise invading pathogens as foreign cells?
- How does a cell stop itself from exploding due to osmosis?
- Why is carbon of such importance in living systems?
- How would you transfer a gene to a plant?
- Explain the mechanism of capillary action.
- What are the advantages of the human genome project?
- How would you locate a gene for a given characteristic in the nucleus of a cell?
- What is the major problem with heart transplants in the receiver?
- Should we be concerned about GMOs? Why or why not?
- Do cellular processes take place at equilibrium?
- How important are primary electrogenic pumps for transmembrane ion transport of organic molecules? Why are these important?
- Why do plants, fungi and bacteria utilise H+ gradients to energise their membranes whereas animals utilise Na+ gradients?

Chemistry

- Questions on organic mechanisms.
- Questions on structure, bonding and energetics.
- Questions on acids and bases.
- Questions on isomerisation.
- Questions on practical chemical analysis.
- Describe the properties of solvents and mechanisms of salvation.

(See also biochemistry questions.)

Classics

- Questions on classical civilisations and literature.
- Why do you think ancient history is important?
- How civilised was the Roman world?
- Apart from your A level texts, what have you read in the original or in translation?

Earth sciences and geology

- Where would you place this rock sample in geological time?
- How would you determine a rock's age?

- Can you integrate this decay curve, and why would the result be useful?
- Questions on chemistry.
- When do you think oil will run out?

Economics

- Explain how the Phillips curve arises.
- Would it be feasible to have an economy that was entirely based on the service sector?
- A man pays for his holiday at a hotel on a tropical island by cheque. He has a top credit rating and rather than cashing it, the hotelier pays a supplier using the same cheque. That supplier does the same thing with one of his suppliers and so on ad infinitum. Who pays for the man's holiday?
- What do you know about the interaction between fiscal and monetary policy?
- I notice that you study mathematics. Can you see how you might derive the profit maximisation formula from first principles?
- Tell me about competition in the television industry.
- How effective is current monetary policy?
- What are your particular interests as regards economics?
- Do you think we should worry about a balance of payments deficit?
- If you were the Chancellor of the Exchequer, how would you maximise tax revenue?
- If you had a fairy godmother who gave you unlimited sums of money, what sort of company would you start and what types of employee would you hire?
- What are the advantages and disadvantages of joining the euro?
- What are the qualities of a good economist?
- Why are you studying economics at A level?
- What would happen to employment and wage rates if the pound depreciated?
- Do you think the Chinese exchange rate will increase?
- How does the housing market affect inflation?
- How has social mobility changed in recent times?
- How best can the government get us out of the recession?

Engineering

- Questions on mathematics and physics, particularly calculus and mechanics.
- Questions on mathematical derivations, for example on laws of motion.
- Look at this mechanical system sitting on my desk – how does it work?
- How do aeroplanes fly?
- What is impedance matching and how can it be achieved?
- How do bicycle spokes work?

- How would you divide a tetrahedron into two identical parts?
- What is the total resistance of the tetrahedron if there are resistors of 1 ohm on each edge?
- How would you design a gravity dam for holding back water?

English

- Why might it be useful for English students to read the *Twilight* series?
- What do you consider to be the most important work of literature of the 20th century?
- Who is your favourite author?
- Apart from your A level texts, what book have you read recently, and why did you enjoy it?
- Give a review of the last play you saw at the theatre.
- Critically analyse this poem.
- Comment in detail on this extract from a novel.
- How has the author used language in this text?

Geography

- Why should it be studied in its own right?
- Is geography just a combination of other disciplines?
- How can cities be made sustainable?
- If I were to visit the area where you live, what would I find interesting?
- Would anything remain of geography if we took the notion of place off the syllabus?
- How important is the history of towns when studying settlement patterns?
- Why is climate so unpredictable?
- What is the importance of space in global warming?
- Why do you think people care about human geography more than physical geography?
- What is more important, mapping or computer models?
- If you went to an isolated island to do research on the beach, how would you use the local community?
- Analyse a graph about a river. Why are there peaks and troughs?
- Look at a world map showing quality of life indicators. Explain the pattern in terms of two of the indicators.

(See also land economy questions.)

History

- Discuss a historical movement that you find particularly interesting.
- How can one define revolution?
- Why did imperialism happen?
- Who was the greater democrat – Gladstone or Disraeli?
- Was the fall of the Weimar Republic inevitable?

- 'History is the study of the present with the benefit of hindsight.' Do you agree?
- Would history be worth studying if it didn't repeat itself?
- What is the difference between modern history and modern politics?
- What is the position of the individual in history?
- Would you abolish the monarchy for ideological or practical reasons?
- Why do historians differ in their views on Hitler?
- What skills should a historian have?
- In what periods has the Holy Grail been popular, with whom and why?
- Why is it important to visit historical sites relevant to the period you are studying?

Human sciences

- Talk about bovine spongiform encephalopathy and its implications, and the role of prions in Creutzfeldt–Jakob disease.
- What causes altitude sickness and how do humans adapt physiologically to high altitudes?
- Tell me about the exploitation of indigenous populations by Westerners.
- Why is statistics a useful subject for human scientists?
- Why are humans so difficult to experiment with?
- How would you design an experiment to determine whether genetics or upbringing is more important?
- What are the scientific implications of globalisation on the world?

Land economy

- Will the UK lose its sovereignty if it joins EMU?
- Will EMU encourage regionalism?
- Will the information technology revolution gradually result in the death of inner cities?
- What has been the effect of the Channel tunnel on surrounding land use?

Law

- Questions on the points of law arising from scenarios – often relating to criminal law or duty of care.
- What does it mean to 'take' another's car?
- A cyclist rides the wrong way down a one-way street and a chimney falls on him. What legal proceedings should he take? What if he is riding down a private drive signed 'no trespassing'?
- X intends to poison his wife but accidentally gives the lethal draught to her identical twin. Would you consider this a murder?
- Questions on legal issues, particularly current ones.
- Should stalking be a criminal offence?
- Should judges have a legislative role?

- Do you think that anyone should be able to serve on a jury?
- Should judges be elected?
- Do judges have political bias?
- To what extent do you think the press should be able to release information concerning allegations against someone?
- Who do you think has the right to decide about euthanasia?
- How does the definition of intent distinguish murder from manslaughter?
- Can you give definitions of murder and manslaughter?
- Should foresight of consequences be considered as intending such consequences?

Material sciences

- Questions on physics, particularly solid materials.
- Questions on mathematics, particularly forces.
- Investigations of sample materials, particularly structure and fractures.

Maths and computation

- Questions (which may become progressively harder) on almost any area of the A level syllabus.

Maths and further maths

- Pure maths questions on integration.
- Applied maths questions on forces.
- Statistics questions on probability.
- Computation questions on iterations, series and computer arithmetic.

Medicine

- What did your work experience teach you about life as a doctor?
- What did you learn about asthma in your work experience on asthma research?
- How have doctors' lives changed in the past 30 years?
- Explain the logic behind the most recent NHS reforms.
- What are the mechanisms underlying diabetes?
- Why is it that cancer cells are more susceptible to destruction by radiation than normal cells?
- How would you determine whether leukaemia patients have contracted the disease because of a nearby nuclear power station?
- What does isometric exercise mean in the context of muscle function?
- What can you tell me about the mechanisms underlying sensory adaptation?
- What is an ECG?
- Why might a general practitioner not prescribe antibiotics to a toddler?

- Why are people anxious before surgery? Is it justifiable?
- How do you deal with stress?
- Why does your heart rate increase when you exercise?
- Questions on gene therapy.
- Questions on the ethics of foetal transplantation.
- Questions on biochemistry and human biology.

Modern languages

Prepare for comprehension and translations and to answer questions on a text given immediately prior to the interview. Also be prepared to have a short conversation in the pre-studied language that you have chosen to study further at university.

- Questions that focus on the use of language in original texts.
- Looking at a poem in the original language and commenting upon it.
- Describe aspects of this poem that you find interesting.
- Interpret this poem, commenting on its tone and context.
- Why do you want to study this language and not another?
- Why is it important to study literature?
- What is the difference between literature and philosophy?
- Questions on cultural and historical context and genre in European literature.
- How important is analysis of narrative in the study of literature?
- How important is knowledge of the biography of the author in the study of their literature?
- What is language?
- Detailed questions on writers, aspects of culture and films mentioned in personal statements.

Natural sciences

- What is an elastic collision?
- What happens when two particles collide – one moving and one stationary?
- What is friction?
- Questions on carboxylic acids.
- What is kinetic energy? How does it relate to heat?

Oriental studies

- What do you know about the Chinese language and its structure?
- What are the differences between English and any oriental language with which you are familiar?
- Does language have an effect on identity?
- Compare and contrast any ambiguities in the following sentences. 'Only suitable magazines are sold here.' 'Many species inhabit a small space.' 'He is looking for the man who crashed his car.'
- Comment on the following sentences. 'He did wrong.' 'He was wrong.' 'He was about to do wrong.'

Philosophy

- What is philosophy?
- Would you agree that if p is true and s believes p, then s knows p?
- Was the question you have just answered about knowing or about the meaning of the word 'know'?
- Comment on these statements/questions: I could be dreaming that I am in this interview; I do not know whether I am dreaming or not; therefore I do not know whether I am in this interview or not. A machine has a free will. When I see red, could I be seeing what you see when you see green?
- Is it a matter of fact or logic that time travels in one direction only?
- Is our faith in scientific method itself based on scientific method? If so, does it matter?
- I can change my hairstyle and still be me. I can change my political opinions and still be me. I can have a sex change and still be me. What is it then that makes me be me?
- Can it ever be morally excusable to kill someone?

Physics

Be prepared to answer any questions relating to the A level syllabus including the following.

- Questions on applied mathematics.
- Questions on mathematical derivations.
- How does glass transmit light?
- How does depressing a piano key make a sound?
- How does the voltage on a capacitor vary if the dielectric gas is ionised?
- How has physics influenced political thinking during the past century?

Politics

- Can you define 'government'? Why do we need governments?
- Can you differentiate between power and authority?
- What makes power legitimate?
- What would be the result of a 'state of nature'?
- How can you distinguish between a society, a state and an economy?
- Will Old Labour ever be revived? If so, under what circumstances?
- What would you say to someone who claims that women already have equal opportunities?
- What would you do tomorrow if you were the leader of the former Soviet Union?
- How does a democracy work?
- What elements constitute the ideologies of the extreme right?
- What do you think of discrimination in favour of female parliamentarians?
- How would you improve the comprehensive system of education?

- Does the UN still have a meaningful role in world affairs?
- Is further EU enlargement sustainable?
- How important is national identity?
- Should medics pay more for their degrees?

Psychology

- Is neuropsychology an exact science? If not, is it useful?
- Questions on the experimental elucidation of the mechanisms underlying behaviour.
- Give some examples of why an understanding of chemistry might be important in psychology.
- A new treatment is tested on a group of depressives, who are markedly better in six weeks. Does this show that the treatment was effective?
- There are records of violent crimes that exactly mimic scenes of violence on television. Does this indicate that television causes real violence?
- Can a robot ever think like a human?
- How would you establish the quietest sound that you can hear as opposed to the quietest sound that you think you can hear?
- Why might one be able to remember items at the beginning and end of an aurally presented list better than items in the middle?
- Could a computer ever feel emotion?
- Is it ethically justifiable to kill animals for the purpose of research?
- What is emotional intelligence?
- Being given data from an experiment and being asked to analyse it.

Sociology

- What is the value of the study of social anthropology?
- Do people need tabloids?
- How would you define terrorism?
- Do you believe in selective education? Are we participating in selective education here?
- Is it possible to pose a sociological problem without sociological bias?
- Does prison work?
- Are MPs only in it for the power?
- How has the study of race and racism changed over the past 20 years?

(See also questions on politics and psychology.)

Theology

- Does moral rectitude reside in the agent, the act or its consequences?
- What, if anything, is wrong with voluntary euthanasia?
- What is the best reason that you can think of for believing in the existence of God?
- Do you think that this course could conceivably be persuasive on the issue?

- What relevance does theology have for art history?
- What relevance does archaeology have for theology?
- Can you comment on the portrayal of Jesus in John versus the other gospels?

Veterinary medicine

- Has your work experience influenced your future career aspirations?
- Can you discuss an aspect of animal physiology which has struck you as contrasting with what you know of human physiology?
- Would our knowledge of BSE have been of value in controlling foot and mouth disease?
- Tell me about the biochemistry of DNA.
- What animal did this skull belong to?

(See also questions on biological sciences and chemistry.)

Any questions?

At the end of the interview you may be asked if you have any questions to ask the interviewer(s). It is always a good idea to have a few questions up your sleeve. One or two is a good number; more than three questions is usually too many. Write them down on a notepad and bring it with you. You will appear professional and keen. You may be able to bring up one of your favourite topics that was not discussed during the main part of the interview.

You probably shouldn't ask about anything that you should know already or about information easily available on the website! This will just make you seem rather dull and certainly not well prepared. Questions such as the following are not likely to impress.

- What will my first year course entail?
- Can I change courses once I'm up at university if I don't like the course I've enrolled on?
- What's special about this college?
- Do I have to live in college?
- Can I choose my room?

If, after all your research, you still have questions about your course or college, this is the time to ask. If there was a topic covered during the interview that you didn't understand, you could enquire about where you can read more about it, or get further clarification from the interviewers themselves. You might also ask for clarification on how you choose course options in your second, third or fourth year or where have last year's graduates ended up; for example, are they undertaking further academic studies, are they working in the City, or have they gone on to business school.

The pooling system

The pooling system exists to ensure that all strong candidates get a good chance of being accepted to an Oxbridge college, but it means something slightly different at Cambridge and Oxford.

At Oxford, you may be 'pooled' after you have had an interview or interviews at your chosen college. This is the reason Oxford keeps applicants for several days during the interview process. You may be seen by other members of the faculty at different colleges during your stay. If you are a particularly strong candidate, academics at several colleges might ask you to interview, even if they are not at the college of your first choice and even if the academics at your preferred college already know they want to offer you a place. More often, being pooled indicates that, although you are a good candidate, your chosen college does not want to offer you a place but another college may. You will then be called for interview at the college that is considering offering you a place.

At Cambridge, pooling happens after the first interview process. If you are a strong candidate but there has been particularly high competition for places at your college, your interviewers may feel that they cannot offer you a place with them but that you deserve a place at Cambridge. They will then place you in the 'pool': a database that can be accessed by members of their faculty at different colleges. Academics at these other colleges, who may have spare places or weaker candidates, will then 'fish out' their choice of strong 'pooled' students and ask them to come for interviews at their college. These second-round or 'pooling' interviews take place at the college of the academic who selects you some time in the second half of December and a few weeks after the first round of interviews. If you are pooled, you still stand a chance of being accepted. At Cambridge, around 887 applicants in the case of the 2014 cycle, about 21% of all offers made, got an offer from a college which was not the one to which they had applied, or a college which was assigned to them because they had made an open application.

Case studies: interview stories from previous applicants

> ### Case study: Eleanor, English Language and Literature, Oxford
>
> The main thing I remember about my interview was that one of my two interviewers asked me to read a poem and respond to it in any way I thought fit. I was given the poem about 20 minutes

before the interview, which was at Oxford. I was fortunate in that I was familiar with the genre and I had already read some poems by the author, W. B. Yeats. As I result, I felt I was able to demonstrate a strong understanding of what to look for in a poem, not just this one, and I was able to use much of the technical language which my teachers had encouraged me to use for literary study. I think the interviewers were pleased with this.

I had prepared myself well by reading widely, but, to be honest, this was not really that difficult for me, as I loved my subject and read widely anyway. I had put a lot of this wider reading into my personal statement, but I had to be selective and include the reading that I really enjoyed and which meant more to me. Fortunately, I was able to talk confidently and knowledgeably about a number of the texts and authors mentioned. I recall being asked to talk at length about my reading of a particular novel, *A Portrait of the Artist as a Young Man*, by James Joyce. I managed to talk in a convincing way about how issues of language and identity helped shape the form and structure of the novel, citing relevant textual evidence to support my case.

My advice to English language and literature students is to read widely well before you are planning your personal statement and to include the texts and authors who have had most impact on you.

I had also prepared myself for the Oxford interview by participating in a summer course organised by the Sutton Trust at Somerville College. This had not only given me an insight into the nature, demand and structure of the English language and literature course at Oxford, but had also confirmed in my own mind that this was the right course for me.

Case study: Seamus, English Language and Literature, Oxford

I went to my interview in Oxford in early December. I was fortunate enough to have a friend to travel with on the train and we also got to talk with students from other schools who were going to have interviews. I had no previous connection to Oxford so I had no idea what to expect. I had seen representations of Oxford on film and television and these had formed my view of what it would be like. The reality was rather more down to earth than my idealistic vision, but that was actually a pleasant surprise in itself.

I met some of the other students who were being interviewed for my subject the evening before the interviews and at breakfast the following morning, which made me feel more relaxed about the whole experience.

There were two interviews at my college. I remember that one of the interviews was with two members of the department. This was quite informal and it was really to find out more about what I had written in my personal statement and what I had done to further my interest in the subject. The next interview was more challenging, however. There was a panel of three interviewers who were much more formal in their approach, so it felt more like a job interview to me. They drilled down deeply into some of the interpretations and assertions I had made in an essay I had had to write a few weeks before. Although I found this interview rather nerve-racking, I was able to justify my opinions with sound arguments and to think on my feet. This was what I thought anyway. To be honest, though, I was not overly confident that I would get offered a place; I just thought that I had done the best I could have done.

I was delighted when I heard in the New Year that my application was successful. My friend got the offer of a place from his college too.

Case study: Olivia, Law, Cambridge

Going to university for me had to be a liberating but secure experience and for that reason I knew I wanted to go to Oxbridge. Liberating in the sense that, academically, I would be surrounded by the brightest minds from around the world. I believed this would allow me to unlock hidden potentials and improve those already discovered. Also for me the tutorial or supervision system at Oxbridge gives security; it would ensure I gained the very best education through close interaction with leaders in my field. More so, the college system appealed as I have been at boarding school for most of my life. I needed that family/community type feel.

Why Cambridge and not Oxford? My exam results! I knew that Cambridge would ask for my UMS (Uniform Mark Scale): as I had scored so high, I was very unlikely not to be interviewed. Moreover, the examining system appealed as it meant the outcome of my degree was spread over three years, as opposed to one big exam at the end of my final year.

Between sending application off and interview, I read the news every day! I also headed the law club at school so I would take controversial excerpts in and we'd debate them – kind of like our own mock interview practice. The interview came; I was ecstatic but I knew a task was at hand. I just focused my thoughts. As clichéd as it sounds, in the two weeks that followed I breathed and lived law cases from the news – I constructed several arguments ready for the Cambridge Law Test. Although most of what I read on didn't come up it made me mentally agile and ready for thinking laterally.

Then the offer came. It was a very tense day. I was abroad, so someone else opened my letter for me. I think I jumped up and down alone for something like 10 minutes before calling my parents, who were in a different country. Honestly, words can't describe the feeling – it's a mixture of elation and a huge sense of responsibility. They think I'm worthy; now I need to prove that I am with my exam results.

Case study: Natasha, Psychology, Philosophy and Linguistics, Oxford

I arrived on Wednesday afternoon to find that I wouldn't have any interviews until Friday, so it's definitely worth bringing some extra reading along with you for some last minute revision and to stop you from sitting around getting stressed. My first interview was mainly for the linguistics part of the course and I was given some basic example sentences and asked to find universal linguistic rules from them. Every rule I came up with was disproven immediately by the interviewer, the aim being for me to re-examine the problem and try again, so don't be put off by this. I was then asked some questions from a psychology tutor, such as could a robot ever think like a human, and could we tell a robot from a human? The tutors were very friendly and were happy to repeat questions or re-word them, so if you're unsure don't be afraid to ask, it's better than rambling on irrelevantly because you don't understand the question!

My second interview was far more intimidating; the tutor was very straight faced and impassive. It seemed as though he was trying to intimidate me; for instance, when I needed help on a logic problem he asked why I didn't get it straight away; then, if I would have got it in a different situation, and so on until eventually I just had to say, 'I guess we will never know now!' Try not to be intimidated by tutors like this, just answer the questions as best you can.

My final interview was at a different college. I had to get myself there so make sure you set off with plenty of time for getting lost, as it was a bit of a maze! Make sure you check that you don't have to be early to the interview room for reading something beforehand, as I was supposed to but didn't know this. Luckily the tutors were late too! In this interview I was shown an experiment about monkeys cracking nuts in Tanzania; I don't think the subject was relevant, more about how I analysed the data, so make sure you read all the pages carefully. Take your time and don't miss a page like I did because I was stressed! After discussing the data I had to devise my own psychology experiment testing some new memory-enhancing device. It was really useful to think of the important factors in biology and chemistry experiments, as it was much the same, things like controlling variables and control groups.

The best preparation in my view was the Oxford reading lists; choose a couple of books from the subject relevant to you, as well as the *New Scientist* for relevant articles, or whatever journal or magazine is specific to your course.

Case study: Kathy, Engineering, Oxford

Mine was an unusual situation, in that I only finally made up my mind to apply for engineering at Oxford about a week before I completed my application. It was not that I was not interested in the subject; in fact, I was passionate about it and I had done related work experience and immersed myself in the subject through wider reading. My A level subjects were also compatible with studying engineering at degree level. However, my family had really wanted me to apply for economics. I toyed with the idea of reading economics and engineering, a new course at the time, but I decided in the end to follow my heart and to aim for engineering.

Once the decision was made, I continued to read widely and to engage in discussing related topics with my teachers. I also had some very useful mock interview practice with my college tutors who were also subject specialists. When I went for the interview, I tried to remain calm and I think this helped a lot.

Although I had been prepared to answer lots of questions, I did not have to say very much during the interview itself. This was because the interviewers mainly gave me problems to do with mathematics and physics; my task was to find solutions to these problems. I think this style of interview was ideal for me. I really felt that I was working with the tutors to achieve a common goal.

I am now in my second year at Oxford. Although it is very hard work, I am very pleased that I decided to apply for engineering.

Case study: Florence, Geography, Oxford

I prepared for my interview by reading my A level notes, but also going beyond this by doing some extra reading around the core subjects. For example, I found the latest Climate Change report from the UN, and memorised key facts from the latest findings so I could use it in my physical geography interview. Having said this, I didn't simply regurgitate the facts, but was able to use them when dealing with questions and incorporate them in a sensible way into my arguments.

I also found that reading the news helped. I had two interviews: in the human geography interview, I was asked to summarise a journal article and talk about issues such as neoliberalism and colonialism in depth. In my physical geography interview, I was asked to describe a map and talk about the trends and patterns I could see.

I thought the process was straightforward, and there weren't any trick questions. They're looking for people who can think clearly, logically and can voice their opinions cogently.

Case study: Lucinda, Theology and Religion, Oxford

You often hear from Oxford and Cambridge interviewees and advisers that the admissions tutors and dons just want to see whether you can think on your feet and whether you are someone with whom they are able to work. They will say that stories of eccentric interviews are a thing of the past. My interviews at Oxford for Theology were rather different and I have vivid memories of them.

The first interview lulled me into a false sense of security. It was with an affable admissions tutor who had a cosy chat with me about many things; the only thing was that none of them was about the subject I wished to study.

The second interview was more daunting. I entered a long, wainscoted chamber, at the other end of which a don was warming himself at a roaring fire. As I approached the welcoming blaze, I was commanded to remain where I was as I had not been invited further into this sacrosanct place. I kept my coat closely fastened as some protection against the icy blast at my end of the room, but was ordered to remove it. Questions about my personal statement were abrasively fired at me. At last, there was some relief. I answered a question which appeared to satisfy my inquisitor. I was rewarded by a long overdue invitation to sit near the hearth and the interrogation became an interview.

My third interview was also a challenge. I was asked to comment upon an unseen passage in Hebrew. Not knowing the language, I requested a translation. The professor seemed impressed by this, declaring, 'At last – someone who admits they can't read Hebrew!' I can only assume that the other poor candidates has struggled valiantly to discuss the passage in the ancient tongue of which they were ignorant.

My ordeal was over. I secured a place at the hallowed halls of Oxford and have never looked back.

The 'post-mortem'

Try not to dwell on how the interview went. Admissions tutors often say that students who think they have done badly in fact have acquitted themselves very well . . . and vice versa. Sometimes a lengthy interview and a good grilling will mean that they've given you a fighting chance to show your true colours.

I like to tell students the story of a candidate who came out of her interview and phoned her school teacher to report back on how her interview had gone. She told him that she had been given a poem to read and analyse and when she went into her interview she announced that she wasn't sure who had written it but she knew by the style of the writing that it had to be a woman. She then spent half her interview justifying her position. The teacher was silent on the other end of the line until he finally confessed that he knew the poem very well and in fact it was written by a man. Cue many tears of frustration and embarrassment.

Three weeks later, this student was offered a place to read English at Oxford. Remember, they are not looking at how much you know now but your potential. Tutors want students who display enthusiasm for their subject, along with a natural flair and ability. They want people who aren't afraid of putting forward their point of view, as long as they can justify it. Ultimately, they want students who will be fun and challenging to teach.

10 | Non-standard applications

This chapter deals with 'non-standard' applications from international students and mature students.

International students

International students are welcome at both Oxford and Cambridge and are valued members of the student population. At Cambridge, there are over 18,000 students at the University, including around 1,300 international students from over 90 different countries reading undergraduate courses.

At Oxford, international students currently come from over 140 countries and make up a third of the student body, including 17% of full-time undergraduate students and 60% of all students.

If you have read the previous chapters in this book, you will know that both universities offer a distinctive form of undergraduate education.

Students apply for a three- or four-year degree in one to three subjects and they study those subjects exclusively. English universities typically do not have 'general education' or 'core curriculum' degrees that, for example, require humanities students to do science courses. The important admissions criterion is excellent academic achievement. Oxford and Cambridge select on academic ability and academic potential, evinced by secondary school results (examination results and/or predicted grades), a personal statement, an academic reference and, if required, an admissions test or written work.

Teaching is by the tutorial system. Students attend lectures and seminars, and have practical laboratory sessions in the sciences, but the heart of the Oxbridge teaching method is a weekly meeting with the student's tutor – typically a leading academic – and one or two other students to engage in an intensive exchange of ideas about the week's work.

All Oxford and Cambridge undergraduates live, eat and study in one of the universities' residential colleges or permanent private halls. These small communities of typically 30–70 academics and 300–500 students from across disciplines are the focus for teaching and for social and sporting life.

Both universities are research intensive, where academics are conducting cutting-edge research in every subject. The collegiate system allows academics and students across subjects and year groups and from different cultures and countries to come together to share ideas.

Oxford and Cambridge qualifications are recognised and valued around the world. Graduates will go on to further study and/or to work in a range of professions in some of the best companies and organisations in the world.

In order to study at Oxford or Cambridge your level of English must be of a high standard. This is measured by your performance in various different examinations, including:

- the IELTS (International English Language Testing System), in which you need a score of at least 7.0 in each section (speaking, listening, writing and reading) – for information about the IELTS exam and where and when it can be taken, visit www.ielts.org
- the English Language GCSE examination at grade B (for Oxford) or C (for Cambridge)
- the TOEFL (Test of English as a Foreign Language) exam, scoring at least 100
- for EU students a high grade in English taken as part of a leaving examination (for example the European Baccalaureate or the Abitur) may be acceptable
- an A grade in the Cambridge Certificate in Advanced English or the Cambridge Certificate of Proficiency in English.

The level of English proficiency required depends a great deal on which subject you wish to study. If you want to apply for an essay-based subject (any of the arts or social science subjects including economics, PPE, psychology, history and English literature) your written work must be fluent. On the other hand, English language is much less important for the study of mathematics. (See www.ox.ac.uk/admissions/undergraduate/international-students/english-language-requirements and www.study.cam.ac.uk/undergraduate/international/requirements.html for further details.)

How much does it cost?

As an international student there are three costs you'll need to consider. These are your tuition fees, college fees and living expenses.

You will have to prove that you can finance yourself for your entire course as it's not possible for you to work during the academic session to pay your way through university. Colleges ask for financial guarantees and proof is also required when applying for a visa.

You will need to be sure of your 'fee status'. Generally speaking, in order to be considered as a 'home' student for tuition fee purposes, you need to either live in an EU member state or have indefinite leave to enter or remain in the UK. In addition, you need to have lived in the European Economic Area (EEA) for the last three years, not solely for educational purposes.

The cost of studying at a UK university for an international student is much higher than for a home student. The tuition fees at Cambridge for the academic year 2015–16 start from £15,063 for most courses, rising to £36,459 for courses in medicine and veterinary medicine (both pre-clinical and clinical training). At Oxford, fees start at £14,845 and rise to £21,855 for courses such as geology, physics and computer science. For more information go to the following websites.

Cambridge:

- international students: www.study.cam.ac.uk/undergraduate/ international
- financial issues for international students: www.study.cam.ac.uk/ undergraduate/international/finance
- electronic application form: www.study.cam.ac.uk/undergraduate/ international/applying.html.

Oxford:

- Student Information and Advisory Service: www.ox.ac.uk/students/ new/international
- official site, including entrance requirements, international qualifica-tions, etc.: www.ox.ac.uk/admissions/graduate/international-students/information-for-applicants
- fees for international students: www.ox.ac.uk/undergraduate/ fees-and-funding/tuition-fees
- international student application forms: www.ox.ac.uk/admissions/ undergraduate_courses/international_applicants/index.html.

College fees

All overseas fee status students, and those UK/EU students who are not eligible for tuition fee support (e.g. because they are taking a sec-ond degree), normally have to pay college fees in addition to university tuition fees. The college fee covers the cost to your college of providing a range of educational, domestic and pastoral services and support. The fees vary slightly between colleges but at Cambridge are typically in the range of £5,500 to £6,500 per year and you should allow for increases in subsequent years. These figures are for 2013–14, so it may well cost more by the time you go to university. At Oxford, the college fees are £6,925 for the academic year 2015–16.

Living expenses

Your living expenses may be higher than for a UK student, for instance if you have to stay in Oxford or Cambridge or the UK during the vacations.

The Oxford website provides the following table which outlines the likely living costs for overseas students in 2014–15; see Table 3 on page 19.

The Cambridge website advises that the minimum resources needed per year are estimated to be approximately £9,200, depending on your lifestyle. However, some of the overseas students I spoke to say that they might not spend as much on social activities as other students. Of course, many international students are likely to spend more money travelling to and from their home countries.

Applying to Oxford or Cambridge

Applications must be made at least three months early, and, with only minor exceptions (e.g. organ scholars), are mutually exclusive for first undergraduate degrees. This means that, in any one year, candidates may apply to only Oxford or Cambridge, not both.

In addition to the usual UCAS application, you will have to submit a Cambridge Online Preliminary Application (COPA). See the website www.study.com.ac.uk/undergraudate/apply/copa.html for more details.

Oxford applicants will have to submit a UCAS application, take a test or occasionally submit written work specific to their chosen subject.

The interview

Every candidate offered a place at Oxbridge will be asked to interview. Normally conducted by a tutor or don, the interview will be used to check whether the course is well suited to the applicant's interests and aptitudes, and to look for evidence of self-motivation, independent thinking, academic potential and ability to learn through the tutorial system.

Cambridge conducts admissions interviews in Canada, Malaysia, Singapore, Hong Kong, China and India for those applicants unable to travel to Cambridge. If it's not possible for you to attend an interview at Oxford in person, it does arrange video conference, telephone and Skype interviews – although this is by no means guaranteed.

Scare stories about impossible questions are rife, but with some advance practice and preparation, the interview should be treated as an opportunity for students to sell themselves rather than as something to be dreaded. Questions are not designed to catch out or embarrass candidates, but to identify intellectual potential and assess how they think and respond to unfamiliar material. To help feel ready, you should practise being in an interview situation and answering questions based around the subject you are looking to study.

Admissions tests

Admissions tests have come to constitute a vital part of many students' applications and are used by Oxbridge and other universities to separate the increasing numbers of students applying with top grades. Tests are now used for several subjects and include the BMAT for medicine and veterinary sciences, the ELAT for English literature and the LNAT for law. Again, the best way for students to prepare for these is practice. Details of these tests are provided in Chapter 8.

Entry requirements vary for international students, so it's always a good idea to read the international pages of each website to ensure you don't miss out. If you don't make the final cut, don't despair. Studying at Oxbridge may be a passport to the realm of the academic elite, but unsuccessful Oxbridge applicants will easily find satisfying and equally challenging alternatives in the UK.

Mature students

A mature student at Oxford or Cambridge is classed as anyone over 21 at the start of October in their first year. Both universities welcome applications from mature students and, like everyone else who wishes to join these highly selective institutions, candidates will need to demonstrate academic ability and a firm commitment to study.

Your work experience and life skills will be considered to be relevant to your application but you must have also undertaken some type of formal academic qualifications within the three years before you apply. You will need to prove to your tutors that you will be able to cope with the demands of academic study and that you have sufficient study skills to commit to an undergraduate degree course. Many different academic qualifications are acceptable. For further information on the qualifications you would need to apply, please consult the universities' websites.

The application procedure for mature students is the same as for other students and you will have to submit an application through UCAS. Also, some subjects require you to take a written test or submit written work as part of your application. Your college will be sympathetic if you are unable to supply appropriate written material but you will need to discuss this with it directly.

Oxford and Cambridge do not accept transfer students under any circumstances. However, you can apply to take a second undergraduate degree. If you're a graduate with an approved degree from another university, you can apply to take a Cambridge BA course as an affiliated student. This means you could take the degree in a year less than usual. At Cambridge, most colleges admit some affiliated students. Some colleges do not admit affiliated students for architecture, and only Lucy Cavendish (women only), St Edmund's and Wolfson consider affiliated applications for medicine or veterinary medicine.

How to apply

Most Cambridge colleges accept some mature students and many have large fellowships and graduate communities that make for a very welcoming and supportive environment. Some students may prefer to apply to one of the four mature-student colleges (Hughes Hall, Lucy Cavendish, St Edmund's and Wolfson). Some colleges will not accept mature students for certain subjects, so you must check their websites carefully.

At Oxford, as a mature student, you can apply to any college. One college (Harris Manchester) and three of the permanent private halls (Blackfriars, St Stephen's House and Wycliffe Hall) take only mature students.

Both universities will be looking for academic potential and motivation just as they do for younger students and they assess each application individually. Mature applicants should not be concerned that their profile will be different. Most mature students who have the right academic background will be called for interview and will be compared fairly against applicants from very different educational backgrounds.

You will need to show evidence of your current academic or work-related performance and give assurance that if you have taken a break from education you are fully back in the routine of dealing with a heavy and challenging academic workload.

Ideally, you will present conventional academic qualifications. If this is not possible or appropriate in your case, the colleges may accept Access, Open University and other Foundation courses. You will need to provide full details of the courses you have taken and the grades achieved and/or predicted when you apply. If you cannot find a way to provide the information on your UCAS form you will need to send appropriate documents (transcripts, mark schemes, etc.) by post at the time you apply.

You will also need to present a reference; this can be written by anybody who is familiar with your current academic work. If you are not currently studying, your referee may be a current or former employer but they must be able to comment on your application and potential.

Mature students from outside the UK should check carefully the information for international students. Because of recent visa changes, if you are considering bringing dependants with you to the UK, it is likely that your dependants will not be eligible for a visa.

Mature students can get information and advice from the admissions offices, as well as details about events and activities run by the universities for prospective mature applicants. See the following websites for more information:

- www.ox.ac.uk/students/new/mature
- www.study.cam.ac.uk/undergraduate/access/mature
- www.ucas.com/how-it-all-works/mature-students.

11 | Getting the letter

Once you've had your interview you will probably have mixed emotions about how well you have done. The majority of students have no strong feeling for whether they are likely to be successful. This is perfectly normal! It's worth remembering that admissions tutors have reported to us that often candidates feel they performed badly at interview when in fact they did very well.

Don't forget, too, that your interview is just one part of your 'package'; before the tutors make a final decision they will consider your application as a whole, which means they will look at your UCAS application and any supplementary questions, school reference, written work and specialist test, as well as your performance at the interview. One tutor told me that at Cambridge they spend about 90 minutes considering every application. They really do their utmost to pick the best candidates and make the whole process as fair as possible.

Oxford decisions are usually sent by the end of January, and conditional offers are nearly always A*A*A*–AAA depending on the subject.

Cambridge decisions are usually received at the beginning of January, although officially they will be posted by the end of January 2016 for those interviewed in 2015. Conditional offers are nearly always A*AA at A level or equivalent. If you have applied through the Cambridge Special Access Scheme you may be made an offer that will take into account your special circumstances.

If you have applied to study mathematics, your offers will be dependent on your grades in two STEPs – three-hour maths exams taken at the end of the A level exam period, which test advanced problem solving and mathematical ingenuity rather than basic knowledge and technique.

Pooled applicants

Some students who applied to Cambridge may find that they have been pooled. This will indicate that they are strong candidates for a place at Cambridge but that there is no place available for them at their chosen college. Approximately 800 to 900 out of around 3,300 of pooled applicants are subsequently awarded a place at Cambridge. Applicants are pooled for a variety of reasons, and are categorised by the pooling college as A (strongly recommended), B (probably worth an offer),

P (outstanding on paper but less impressive at interview) or S (applicant in need of reassessment).

Sometimes a college wishes to see other applicants from the pool before it fills all of its places with direct applicants – this sometimes results in several applicants being pooled and subsequently being awarded places at their original college of choice. Some are subsequently invited for interview at other colleges; if this happens the college concerned will contact you to ask you to come for an interview early in January. If another college wishes to offer you a place following the pool, you should hear from them at the start or middle of January. Otherwise, your original college will write back to you by the end of January informing you that you have been unsuccessful.

Rejection

If you are unsuccessful at either university, you will receive a rejection letter in the post between December and mid-January. If this is the case for you, do not despair. Remember that there is incredibly high competition to get a place at Oxbridge. Although for many subjects one in five students interviewed are accepted, for other subjects 10 students are interviewed for one place. More than 5,000 of the unsuccessful applicants per year will have been predicted three As or higher at A level, and are clearly intelligent and successful students.

If you are rejected, despite having a set of perfect grades and impeccable references, and you want to know why, ring the admissions tutor at your chosen college and ask for feedback. If your grades are good and you are really set on claiming a place at Oxbridge, think about why you did not succeed the first time and try again. Neither Cambridge nor Oxford looks badly on students who apply twice. You may have been too young the first time or too focused on school exams to dedicate enough time to the application process. Alternatively, you may not have made an appropriate subject choice and were not passionate enough about your field. If once was enough, however, focus on your other university choices and draw on your Oxbridge experiences to help you in your preparation for future interviews.

If you don't get the grades required

If you did not get the grades required by Oxbridge (for example you got an AAB rather than A*AA), your conditional offer will be withdrawn. You may wish to contact the admissions tutor at your college at this point, but you should be prepared for the fact that it is unlikely you will get a second chance. Oxford and Cambridge do not look kindly on retake students, unless of course there is a real and significant reason why you did not fulfil your potential in the exams (for example, illness or a bereavement in the family).

UCAS has an 'Adjustment' system where students who get above their predicted grades can go back to universities who rejected them and try for a place again. However, it is unlikely that this system will apply to Oxford and Cambridge since they are always extremely oversubscribed. What you can do if your exam results exceed your expectations is to reapply the following year with your excellent grades.

Remember, if you are a motivated and focused student, then you will excel at whatever university you go to, and if you love your subject, then your interest will flourish wherever you are.

Case study: Charlie, Hertford College, Oxford

I initially applied to a college in Oxford to read History. I performed well in the interview, but did not get an offer, although the rejection letter still reassured me that I had been a strong candidate; it was simply that I was out-performed by the other applicants. I went on to get excellent A level grades.

The rejection gave me a chance to reflect on what I really wanted to study at university. I had always been interested in English Literature, but had not studied it at A level. Poetry has always been my favourite genre and I have been writing poetry in earnest since my early teens. In fact, I had a volume of poetry published during my enforced gap year. This led to a series of visits to schools and even prisons, where I gave readings from my book and discussed my work. Clearly, this augmented my confidence; it also crystallised my desire to study English Language and Literature at university and to reapply to Oxford in order to achieve this aim.

The following year I enrolled on a one-year intensive A level course in English Literature. I thoroughly enjoyed the inspiring lessons given by my teacher and got on really well with my classmates. I finished the year with the top grade. Before reapplying to Oxford in the autumn term, I rang around the various colleges to see how they would view me as a candidate applying the second time around. Having heard about my profile, a surprising number said they would view my application favourably. I got my place; I am so glad I persevered.

Appendix 1: timetables

The year before you apply

March

- Request an undergraduate prospectus and the alternative prospectus from the student unions of Cambridge or Oxford.
- Research other universities to which you are considering applying.

April

- Write the first draft of your personal statement.
- Go to an open day.
- Book a place at an open day.

June

- Sit your AS levels (or equivalent exams).
- Oxford open days on 1st and 2nd.
- Cambridge open days on 2nd and 3rd.

Summer holidays

- Ask friends and family to read your personal statement and make revisions.
- Do some work experience.

The year in which you apply

September

- Finalise your personal statement with your teachers.
- Visit the UCAS website (www.ucas.com) and register.
- Fill in the UCAS form (UCAS applications may be submitted from mid- September). (www.ucas.com/apply-and-track/key-dates)
- Register and book a place to sit the LNAT (if you want to study law at Oxford). (www.lnat.ac.uk)

- Register for the BMAT if you are applying for medicine (at Oxford or Cambridge) or veterinary science (Cambridge only). (www.admissionstestingservice.org/for-test-takers/bmat.dates-dates-and-costs/)
- Register for other subject-related tests.
- Oxford open day on 18 September.

October

- For Oxford applicants register and book LNAT test on 5th. Deadline for sitting the test is 20 October at the latest (although 2015 deadline may change).
- The deadline for UCAS receiving your application, whether for Oxford or Cambridge, is 6p.m. on 15 October.
- The deadline for subject-related tests is 15 October.
- Fill in the separate Cambridge SAQ. This will be emailed to you and must be completed by 22 October (although the 2015 deadline may change).
- Receive the acknowledgement letter from your chosen college in mid to late October.

November

- Sit the BMAT in the first week of November if you are applying for medicine (at Oxford or Cambridge) or veterinary science (Cambridge only).
- Sit subject-related tests (although the 2015 deadline may change).
- Receive the letter inviting you to interview from Oxford or Cambridge and explaining if and when to submit written work. Alternatively, you may receive a letter rejecting you at this point.
- Submit written work with the special form – see faculty website for details. (Work should be sent directly to the college unless you have made an 'open application', in which case send it directly to the faculty. The work should be marked by your school). For Oxford the dedline is 10 November. For Cambridge it is 15 November.

December

- If invited, attend interviews in the first three weeks of December (see precise interview dates for your subject in the prospectus).
- You may have to sit some tests at interview.
- At Cambridge you may have to sit the TSA.

January

- Beginning of January: applicants who have been placed in the 'winter pool' are notified (Cambridge only). This may or may not entail going to Cambridge for another set of interviews.
- Hear the outcome of your application from Oxford by 7 January.
- End of January: hear the outcome of your application from Cambridge.

June

- Sit A levels (or equivalent exams).
- After A levels sit STEP or AEA (maths only).

August

- Mid-August: results day.
- If you have made your grades your place will be confirmed by the university.
- If you have not made your grades, contact the admissions tutor of your college.
- You may be sent a letter of rejection at this point.

Appendix 2: glossary

Admissions tutor
The tutor especially assigned the role of selecting candidates.

Alumni
People who once went to the college but who have now graduated.

Bedder
The person who cleans your room at Cambridge.

Clearing
When the A level exam results come out in August, students who do not make their offers or, alternatively, students who get much better grades than predicted, can enter the competition for places at universities that have spare places.

Collections
Exams sat at the beginning of each term at Oxford in the colleges.

Collegiate system
This term describes the fact that both Oxford and Cambridge universities are divided into about 30 separate colleges, where students live and where their social lives are based.

Deferred entry
This means you would like to take a gap year (i.e. defer your entry for a year). You apply this year but will accept a place in two years' time.

Deselected
Some candidates will not make it to the interview; they are 'deselected' before the interview and will receive a letter of rejection.

Director of studies (DOS)
Your DOS at Cambridge University is an academic member of staff from your subject faculty who is also a fellow of your college. He or she is responsible for your academic development and will meet with you at the beginning and end of each term to check on your progress and will probably be your interviewer. The DOS at Cambridge is the equivalent to a tutor at Oxford.

Don
A teacher at a university; in particular a senior member of an Oxbridge college.

Exhibition
A scholarship you can win in recognition of outstanding work at Oxford.

Faculty
The department building dedicated to one particular subject, for example, the Faculty of Architecture.

Fellow
An academic member of a college. Each academic in every faculty is also assigned a college; this is where their office space is located. Some more senior fellows are given responsibility for the academic achievement of the students at their college and act as the DOS (at Cambridge) or tutor (at Oxford) of a number of undergraduates.

Fresher
First-year undergraduate student.

Go up
Traditionally, instead of simply saying 'go to university', for Oxford and Cambridge the term used is to 'go up' to university.

Hall
One of the places where you eat your meals in college. Usually you will be offered a three-course evening meal with wine. Formal hall is a more elaborate affair and you may be required to wear your gown.

Junior common room (JCR)
A common room for all undergraduate students of a given college. Each college has its own JCR.

Norrington table
Oxford league table that measures each college's academic achievement at the final examinations.

Open application
A way of applying to either Oxford or Cambridge without specifying a college.

Oxbridge
The collective term for Oxford and Cambridge.

Permanent private halls
These are like mini-colleges in Oxford. Two of them – St Benet's Hall (men only) and Regent's Park College (men and women) – are for students studying any subject, but the remaining five are mainly for people who are training to be in the ministry.

Pool
The pool is where applicants who are rejected by their first-choice college are held until another college selects them for an interview. The other college may do this for a variety of reasons, such as if they do not

have enough good applicants and want to find better ones, or if they want to check that their weakest chosen student is better than another college's rejected student – a sort of moderation process.

Porter's lodge
Your first port of call at an Oxford or Cambridge college. This is where post gets delivered and where, if you get lost, they will be able to direct you – a bit like reception.

Porters
The men and women who act like wardens of the lodge.

Read
Instead of 'studying' a subject, the verb used is to 'read' a subject.

Scholar
Scholarships are usually awarded at the end of the first year for outstanding work. Oxford scholars get to wear a more elaborate gown and are given a small financial bursary (usually around £200 a year). Music scholars hold their award for the whole time they are at univeroity.

Scout
The person who cleans your room at Oxford.

Subfusc
The black gown, black trousers/skirt, white shirt and black tie Oxford students must wear to take exams.

Summon
Another way to say 'to be called' for interview.

Supervision
A class held on a one-to-one basis or in a small group with your tutor (at Cambridge).

Supplementary Application Questionnaire (SAQ)
This is sent out by Cambridge once you have submitted your UCAS application. The SAQ gives Cambridge more information about you and your application and must be submitted within one week after you receive it. The SAQ is filled out online and costs nothing to send; if you do not have access to email you can contact the Cambridge admissions office for a paper version.

Tompkins table
Cambridge league table that measures each college's academic achievement at the final examinations.

Tripos
Term used to describe Cambridge degree courses being divided into blocks of one or two years, called Part I and Part II.

Tutor

At Oxford, your tutor is an academic member of staff from your subject faculty, who is also a fellow of your college. He or she is responsible for your academic development and will meet with you on a regular basis to check on your progress, and will probably be your interviewer. The DOS at Cambridge is the equivalent to a tutor at Oxford.

Tutorial

A class held on a one-to-one basis or in a small group with your tutor (at Oxford).

Viva voce

An oral exam given when you are being considered for a First Class degree and the examiners want to ask you further questions about your exam papers.

Appendix 3: Norrington and Tompkins tables

Table 4 Norrington Table – Oxford 2013–2014

College	Score	Rank
Merton	74.70%	1
St John's	74.56%	2
Worcester	73.98%	3
New	73.96%	4
Wadham	73.79%	5
Jesus	73.76%	6
Hertford	73.33%	7
Harris Manchester	72.59%	8
Magdalen	72.18%	9
Lincoln	72.13%	10
Trinity	71.94%	11
St Catherine's	71.73%	12
St Anne's	71.58%	13
Corpus Christi	71.52%	14
Exeter	71.29%	15
Christ Church	71.11%	16
St Hugh's	70.99%	17
Keble	70.53%	18
Brasenose	70.09%	19
Balliol	70.09%	20
St Hilda's	69.75%	21
St Peter's	69.48%	22
Oriel	69.02%	23
University	68.85%	24
Mansfield	68.47%	25
Lady Margaret Hall	68.32%	26
Somerville	68.22%	27
St Edmund Hall	68.13%	28
Queen's	68.00%	29
Pembroke	63.14%	30

Source: https://en.wikipedia.org/wiki/Norrington_Table
Reprinted under CC-BY-SA (http://creativecommons.org/licenses/by-sa/3.0/)

Table 5 Tompkins table – Cambridge (2014)

Position	College	Score	% of Firsts
1 (1)	Trinity	74.53%	42.9%
2 (2)	Pembroke	71.56%	36.2%
3 (3)	Trinity Hall	70.18%	32.7%
4 (6)	Jesus	68.79%	29.7%
5 (4)	Emmanuel	68.78%	29.4%
6 (5)	Churchill	68.77%	31.1%
7 (7)	Queen's	68.35%	27.2%
8 (11)	Clare	67.63%	29.2%
9 (8)	Christ's	67.62%	24.8%
10 (15)	Magdalene	67.21%	25.8%
11 (12)	Downing	66.99%	26.2%
12 (10)	Peterhouse	66.49%	26.5%
13 (18)	Selwyn	66.28%	24.3%
14 (14)	King's	66.22%	25.0%
15 (17)	Gonville & Caius	66.21%	25.2%
16 (13)	St John's	65.84%	24.9%
17 (19)	Sidney Sussex	64.77%	21.2%
18 (16)	Corpus Christi	64.47%	21.8%
19 (20)	Fitzwilliam	64.36%	21.4%
20 (22)	Robinson	64.28%	20.3%
21 (9)	St Catharine's	64.28%	20.7%
22 (23)	Newnham	62.20%	18.4%
23 (21)	Girton	61.13%	16.4%
24 (26)	Homerton	59.99%	13.8%
25 (25)	Wolfson	59.55%	16.8%
26 (24)	Murray Edwards	59.17%	10.3%
27 (27)	Hughes Hall	58.73%	12.7%
28 (29)	St Edmund's	58.49%	14.8%
29 (28)	Lucy Cavendish	54.08%	11.1%

Figure in brackets shows previous year's position.
Source: https://en.wikipedia.org/wiki/Tompkins_Table

Appendix 4: maps

Oxford map

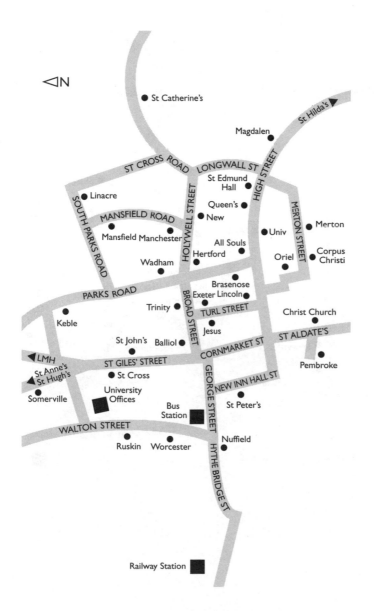

Cambridge map